# MEDAL OF HONOR
## PACIFIC ASSAULT™

**PRIMA** OFFICIAL GAME GUIDE          **KENNETH** MILLER

Prima Games
A Division of Random House, Inc.

3000 Lava Ridge Court
Roseville, CA 95661
1-800-733-3000
www.primagames.com

Product Manager: Jill Hinckley
Project Editor: Amanda Peckham
Design & Layout: Derek Hocking, Simon Olney

Important:
Prima Games has made every effort to determine that the information contained in this book is accurate. However, the publisher makes no warranty, either expressed or implied, as to the accuracy, effectiveness, or completeness of the material in this book; nor does the publisher assume liability for damages, either incidental or consequential, that may result from using the information in this book. The publisher cannot provide information regarding game play, hints and strategies, or problems with hardware or software. Questions should be directed to the support numbers provided by the game and device manufacturers in their documentation. Some game tricks require precise timing and may require repeated attempts before the desired result is achieved.

ISBN: 0-7615-4330-9
Library of Congress Catalog Card Number: 2003114653
Printed in the United States of America

04 05 06 07 LL 10 9 8 7 6 5 4 3 2 1

# MEDAL OF HONOR
## PACIFIC ASSAULT™

PRIMA OFFICIAL GAME GUIDE

# CONTENTS

# BASICS

## MOVEMENT

### Running

When moving around while standing up, you run at full speed. This is dangerous when there are soldiers in the vicinity, so it's better to crouch. Run only when traversing an already cleared area or when quickly ducking for cover in the middle of a firefight.

### Crouching/Prone

To go from standing to crouching, press the Crouch key once. If you press the key again from crouching, you'll go prone. Pressing the Jump key moves you up by one degree (from prone to crouching or from crouching to standing). Finally, you can press the Prone key to go immediately to the prone position.

Crouching makes you much harder to hit than when you are simply standing around. You can move slowly while crouching. This allows you to stay low and avoid detection when exploring enemy territory. Crouching also makes most cover much more effective because rocks and other obstructions are rarely as tall as you are.

If you need to go even lower than a crouch, go prone. You're very hard to see when prone, but it also greatly reduces your movement speed. Most of the time, simply crouching will be enough.

> **TIP:** UNLESS YOU'RE CERTAIN YOU'VE CLEARED OUT AN AREA AND IT'S SAFE, IT'S BEST TO STAY IN THE CROUCH POSITION AT ALL TIMES.

### Cover

Staying behind cover means staying alive. Learning to find and use cover in the field is a very important technique.

When you're deep in the jungle, rocks and trees make the best cover. In enemy encampments, use buildings and sandbags as cover. Often, your own men will seek out the best cover, so following them is a good idea.

# WEAPONS

## Aiming

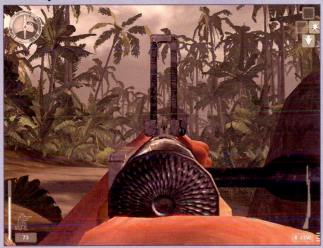

Hold the Aim key to change your view to your gun's sights (or scope). Aiming allows you to land a more precise shot as well as giving you a short-range zoom. You move very slowly while aiming, so take your shot quickly unless you're safely covered.

## Shooting

You can't run around, firing wildly, and expect to get much done. Not only is it important to aim carefully, it's also essential to know how your weapon fires and how long it takes to chamber a new round. Moving greatly reduces your accuracy, so stay still, crouch, and squeeze off each shot like it means something.

## Reloading

Keep your gun fully loaded whenever possible. Running out of bullets in the thick of battle can mean a gruesome end for poor Tommy. Any time you're free from enemy fire, reload your gun; even if you've only fired a few bullets, it never hurts to be prepared. This is especially true with guns that are slow to reload.

## Enemy Weapons

When you take down an enemy soldier, he often drops his weapon onto the ground. If you approach the weapon, you can switch it for your current one by pressing the Use key. If you're happy with your current weapon (and have plenty of ammo), then hang onto it. However, if you wish you had a rifle instead of a submachine gun, grab that gun and use the enemy's weapon against him.

## OTHER INFORMATION

### Your Squad

On every mission after Pearl Harbor, you travel (and fight) with a squad. These teammates are often the difference between life and death, as they frequently yell out updates and suggestions. Listen carefully for your men to tell you there are incoming enemies or grenades, that the area is secure, or that you've reached your objective destination. Of course, your squad also adds firepower during a fight. They're not particularly accurate or quick on the trigger, however, so don't rely on them too heavily to do your dirty work.

### *Medic*

Perhaps the most important man on your team is the medic. If you're injured, you can call the medic to your side to patch you up to full health. The healing isn't instantaneous, though, so make sure you're in a safe spot before you yell out to him.

> **NOTE:** THE NUMBER OF TIMES YOU CAN USE THE MEDIC IS LIMITED, SO WAIT UNTIL YOUR HEALTH IS AS LOW AS YOU CAN STOMACH BEFORE YOU CALL HIM OVER.

### Vehicles

In most missions, your exposure to vehicles will be when enemy tanks are firing at you. Whenever possible, use placed machine guns or other artillery to destroy the enemy vehicles. If necessary, use your own small arms to do the job.

In rare cases, you and your men will take control of your own vehicle to get to a destination or clear an area out quickly. When you're in a vehicle, a new life bar appears next to your own, indicating the amount of damage the vehicle can take before it is destroyed. If you're protecting a friendly vehicle, keep a close eye on this gauge.

## Mission Objectives

At the beginning of each mission (and at other times throughout), you are given objectives to complete. Watch for text that says, "An objective has been added." Keep track of your current objectives by pressing `TAB`. You can tell if you've cleared the area, destroyed the right artillery, or shot down enough planes by watching for your objectives to update.

When looking for objective targets, watch for a glowing red icon. This indicates an item you can manipulate to complete an objective.

### The Compass

Your compass always points toward your current objective. The path may not always be straight and narrow. Often, you must navigate around objects and enemy soldiers to reach the objective. The compass also shows the general distance to your objective with a ball on each side of the arrow. The closer you are, the closer the balls move toward the arrow.

The locations of your teammates (and the medic, specifically) are also indicated on your compass.

### Combat Squad Control

In the upper right corner of the screen is a collection of four icons. This represents your Combat Squad Control. Each of the icons represents a command you can give to your squad during battle. To issue a command, press the arrow key on your keyboard that corresponds to the position of the icon.

| Direction | Command |
|---|---|
| Up | Move forward |
| Down | Fall back |
| Left | Assemble |
| Right | Covering fire |

**NOTE:** IF ONE OR MORE OF THE ICONS SHOWS A RED X WHEN YOU PRESS THAT KEY, YOU CANNOT GIVE THAT COMMAND AT THAT TIME.

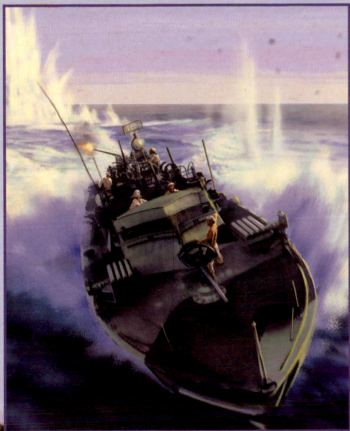

# WEAPONS

## Allied

### Smith and Wesson M1917 .45 Magnum Revolver

**Ammo Type:** U.S. Pistol
**Rate of Fire:** Fast
**Round Capacity:** 6
**Max Ammo:** 100
**Alt Fire:** Pistol Whip
**Weight:** 2.25 pounds
**Date entered into production:** October 1917

**Description:** Classic six shooter. Smooth walnut grip. Limited ammo but great stopping power. Gun is reloaded with two 3-round "half moon" clips. Soldiers generally carried ammo pouches with 18 extra rounds.

**Gameplay Notes:** As you'd expect, the Magnum has poor accuracy at long-range, but it's great for taking down enemy soldiers at close-range.

### Colt .45

**Ammo Type:** U.S. Pistol
**Rate of Fire:** Fast
**Round Capacity:** 7
**Max Ammo:** 100
**Alt Fire:** Pistol Whip
**Weight:** 2.4 pounds
**Date entered into production:** 1911

**Description:** The most famous American handgun of World War II was the Model 1911 .45-caliber semiautomatic pistol invented by John M. Browning. This pistol was born out of the U.S. military's frustration with the limited stopping power of smaller-caliber revolvers during the Spanish-American War. Both Colt and the Springfield Armory produced the pistol between 1911 and 1915, and by the end of World War I, over 60 percent of the American soldiers in France were issued Colt 45s. After World War I, slight modifications were made to the trigger, hammer, grip, and frame. Although it was issued to officers and squad leaders, the Colt was not standard issue for infantrymen during World War II. This didn't keep many front-line soldiers from obtaining them, and the regulation against their carrying pistols was rarely enforced. The Colt was recognized as a weapon of last resort—most soldiers had more effective weapons available, but no one denied the feeling of security the weighty Colt 45 provided. It remained the standard U.S. sidearm until 1984.

**Gameplay Notes:** The Colt .45 is similar to the .45 Magnum, but its higher ammo count and accuracy make it a slightly better weapon.

### .30 Caliber M1 Carbine Rifle

**Ammo Type:** U.S. Rifle
**Rate of Fire:** Fast
**Round Capacity:** 15
**Max Ammo:** 200
**Alt Fire:** Rifle Butt Bash
**Weight:** 5 pounds
**Date entered into production:** August 1941 (and in much larger numbers in October 1941)

**Description:** The M1 Carbine was intended to "fill the gap" between the 9+ pound, full power M1 Garand rifle and the capable, but limited by its caliber, M1911A1 pistol. At any range but point-blank, the Carbine was easier to hit with than the pistol. More than 6 million Carbines were produced by a plethora of contractors, from hardware manufacturers to jukebox companies.

**Gameplay Notes:** The M1 has a great ammo capacity and a quick rate of fire, but its stopping power is low. It takes several shots to take down an enemy unless your headshot accuracy is top-notch.

## Springfield M1903 Rifle

**Ammo Type:** U.S. Rifle
**Rate of Fire:** Slow
**Round Capacity:** 5-round internal box magazine
**Max Ammo:** 200
**Alt Fire:** Rifle Butt Bash
**Weight:** 8.69 pounds
**Date entered into production:** 1903

**Description:** The most common rifle by far during the first half of the war. This in reality is the only rifle the Marines used with any regularity until the Carbine and Garand became available to them in '43. Loaded with 5-round stripper clips or one round at a time.

**Gameplay Notes:** The Springfield is essentially the opposite of the M1 Carbine. Its round capacity is low and its rate of fire is slow, but a well-aimed headshot or a couple body shots will drop an enemy.

## Springfield M1903/A5 Sniper Rifle

**Ammo Type:** U.S. Rifle
**Rate of Fire:** Slow
**Round Capacity:** 5-round internal box magazine
**Max Ammo:** 200
**Alt Fire:** Rifle Butt Bash
**Weight:** 8.69 pounds
**Date entered into production:** 1903

**Description:** An early sniper rifle that was used until the M1903A1/Unertl came about. Historically not very accurate and with a weak scope. These saw service until they were widely replaced in the second half of the war.

**Gameplay Notes:** Historical lack of accuracy notwithstanding, the inclusion of the scope makes the Springfield Sniper Rifle useful for hitting distant targets. Obviously, its slow rate of fire is not ideal for standard mid-range firefights.

## M1 Garand (With Bayonet)

**Ammo Type:** U.S. Rifle
**Rate of Fire:** Fast
**Round Capacity:** 8
**Max Ammo:** 200
**Alt Fire:** Bayonet Stab
**Weight:** 9.5 pounds
**Date entered into production:** 1936

**Description:** The "U.S. Rifle, Caliber .30, M1 rifle" (or Garand) was the standard-issue rifle for American infantry. Named after its inventor, John C. Garand, it was the first semiautomatic rifle widely used in combat. Although it was adopted by the Army in 1936, the Garand was in short supply until 1943, but by the end of the war more than 4 million had been produced. The Garand was easy to disassemble and clean, and its combination of caliber, muzzle velocity, and semiautomatic operation provided superior firepower over bolt-action rifles. Its only weakness was that partially fired clips were so difficult to reload that GIs tended to simply fire off the remaining rounds and insert a new clip.

**Gameplay Notes:** The Garand is an excellent rifle (when you can get your hands on it). The semiautomatic firing gives it a fairly quick rate of fire and it's quick to reload. The attached bayonet also allows it to double as an effective close-quarters weapon if the situation calls for it.

> **NOTE:** UNLIKE THE REST OF THE HAND-HELD WEAPONS, YOU CANNOT MANUALLY RELOAD THE GARAND. WHEN YOU FIRE ALL EIGHT ROUNDS, YOU RELOAD AUTOMATICALLY.

## Model 11 Remington Semi-Automatic Riot Gun

**Ammo Type:** U.S. Shotgun
**Rate of Fire:** Slow
**Round Capacity:** 5
**Max Ammo:** 100
**Alt Fire:** Rifle Butt Bash
**Weight:** 7.6 pounds
**Date entered into production:** 1941

**Description:** Semi-Automatic shotgun, useful in close combat situations. Blue tinted steel gives it a unique look. "U.S." and a flaming bomb stamped on the left side.

**Gameplay Notes:** The Remington is a beast in close-quarters. It fires and reloads slowly, but against single targets, this won't be a problem. Obviously, when facing enemies at anything beyond close-range, switch to another weapon.

## M1928A1 Thompson Submachine Gun with 30 Round Magazine/50 Round Drum

**Ammo Type:** U.S. SMG
**Rate of Fire:** 600–725 rpm
**Round Capacity:** 30/50
**Max Ammo:** 500
**Alt Fire:** Rifle Butt Bash
**Weight:** 11 pounds
**Date entered into production:** 1940

**Description:** John T. Thompson, who helped develop the M1903 Springfield rifle and M1911 .45 caliber pistol, began work on a "trench broom" for close quarter combat shortly after his retirement from the Army in 1918. He recognized that the .45 caliber slug used in the M1911 pistol would be devastating when used in a fully automatic weapon. One of the main assets of the Thompson submachine gun was reliability; it performed better than most submachine guns when exposed to dirt, mud, and rain. The main complaints against the Thompson were its weight, inaccuracy at ranges over 50 yards, and lack of penetrating power.

**Gameplay Notes:** At close-range, the Thompson is a great addition to your arsenal. Its high ammo capacity (especially in the 500-round model) allows you to drop several targets in a row. However, because you'll carry out most fighting at mid- to long-range, the Thompson will probably spend more time in your backpack than in your hands.

## Reising Model 55 SMG

**Ammo Type:** U.S. SMG
**Rate of Fire:** 400–450 rpm
**Round Capacity:** 20
**Max Ammo:** 500
**Alt Fire:** Rifle Butt Bash
**Weight:** 6 pounds
**Date entered into production:** 1941

**Description:** The main benefit to the M55 was its weight and size. Small and compact, they could be stowed where most weapons wouldn't fit. Its light weight enabled soldiers to move with almost total freedom while wielding the weapon. However, the weapon was prone to malfunction, and when the Thompson became more widely available, the Reising became a thing of the past.

**Gameplay Notes:** The Reising is similar to the Thompson, but as the description implies, it is generally an inferior weapon. In-game, its drawbacks are its smaller ammo capacity and slower rate of fire. The weapon's light weight does allow you to move at full speed while carrying it, however.

**TIP:** BOTH SUBMACHINE GUNS HAVE A BRIGHT MUZZLE FLASH AND LOSE ACCURACY RAPIDLY WHEN FIRED FULL-AUTO. FIRE IN BURSTS TO ALLEVIATE THESE PROBLEMS AS MUCH AS POSSIBLE.

## 1941 Johnson Light Machine Gun (Director's Ed. Only)

**Ammo Type: U.S. MG**
**Rate of Fire: 400 rpm**
**Round Capacity: 20**
**Max Ammo: 500**
**Alt Fire: Rifle Butt Bash**
**Weight: 13 pounds**
**Date entered into production: mid-1941**

**Description:** Very unique light machine gun, used by many special ops Marine outfits such as the Raiders. Single rounds (or a 5-round stripper clip) could be added to the right side of the gun without removing the main magazine, allowing for reloading on the fly or the addition of tracer rounds.

**Gameplay Notes:** This machine gun has a small bipod mounted toward the end of the barrel, which automatically extends if you use this weapon while prone. It's fairly lightweight so you can run as fast as you can with a Thompson, but it has more stopping power.

## Browning Automatic Rifle (BAR)

**Ammo Type: U.S. MG**
**Rate of Fire: 500 rpm**
**Round Capacity: 20**
**Max Ammo: 500**
**Alt Fire: Rifle Butt Bash**
**Weight: 18.5 pounds**
**Date entered into production: 1918**

**Description:** The initial M1918A1 version of the Browning automatic rifle (BAR) was first used in combat by American soldiers during World War I, and many of these guns saw service in World War II. The BAR received high praise for its reliability under adverse conditions. In 1940, model M1918A2 was adopted. Unlike earlier models, it could only be fired in two automatic modes—slow (300 to 450 rounds per minute) or fast (500 to 650 rounds per minute)—but not in semiautomatic mode. Both versions were widely used; the BAR was a popular weapon in all theaters because it was reliable and offered an excellent combination of rapid fire and penetrating power. The BAR's only serious drawback was its lack of a quick-change barrel to reduce the chances of overheating.

**Gameplay Notes:** The weight of this weapon presents its main strength and weakness. It has great stopping power (especially at mid-range) but it also noticeably slows your movement speed while carrying it.

## Mark II Hand Grenade

**Ammo Type: U.S. Grenade**
**Delay: 5 seconds**

**Description:** Typical front-line Allied infantry fragmentation grenade.

**Gameplay Notes:** Grenades are useful for clearing out entrenched soldiers or just scaring the enemy out of hiding. Holding down the trigger primes the grenade, and shortly a ticking sound begins, indicating when the grenade will explode. Let go of the trigger to throw the grenade.

## Japanese

### Nambu Model 8mm Pistol

**Ammo Type: Japanese Pistol**
**Rate of Fire: Fast**
**Round Capacity: 8**
**Max Ammo: 100**
**Alt Fire: Pistol Whip**
**Weight: 2 pounds**

**Description:** This is a semiautomatic, recoil-operated magazine-fed hand weapon. Japanese markings on the right side read "Nambu Model."

**Gameplay Notes:** This weapon lacks the firepower of the Allied pistols, but it has a quick rate of fire and reload time.

### Model 38 6.5mm Arisaka Rifle (With Bayonet)

**Ammo Type: Japanese Rifle**
**Rate of Fire: Slow**
**Round Capacity: 5-round cartridge**
**Max Ammo: 200**
**Alt Fire: Bayonet Stab**
**Weight: 9.08 pounds**

**Description:** This gun was turn bolt operated and loaded with 5-round stripper clips (a flat metal piece holding a 5-round stack, which was inserted at the top of the magazine, the rounds thumbed down into position, and the metal piece sent flying when the bolt was closed). These rifles had light recoil and little muzzle flash. Although of light hitting power, the 6.5mm rounds tumbled in flight and broke up upon impact, causing great damage.

**Gameplay Notes:** This is the weapon the Japanese soldiers most commonly carry. As a result, you will spend most of your time using the Arisaka as your weapon. It's slow to fire and reload, but its good accuracy and firepower more than make up for it. The bayonet also makes the Arisaka an excellent close-range weapon.

### Model 44 Cavalry Carbine Rifle (With Bayonet)

**Ammo Type: Japanese Rifle**
**Rate of Fire: Slow**
**Round Capacity: 5-round cartridge**
**Max Ammo: 200**
**Alt Fire: Bayonet Stab**
**Weight: 11.75 pounds w/bayonet**

**Description:** Standard carbine rifle with permanently attached folding bayonet.

**Gameplay Notes:** The Model 44 is similar to the Arisaka when it comes to rate of fire, but the heavier weight slows you down while carrying it.

## Model 97 6.5 mm Sniper Rifle

**Ammo Type: Japanese Rifle**
**Rate of Fire: Slow**
**Round Capacity: 5**
**Max Ammo: 200**
**Alt Fire: Rifle Butt Bash**
**Weight: 9.75 pounds**

**Description:** A fairly typical 6.5mm rifle with a scope mounted on the left side of the receiver.

**Gameplay Notes:** The Model 97 is a pretty even counterpart to the Allied Springfield rifle. Use the scope to deal with long-range targets.

## Type 100 Submachine Gun

**Ammo Type: Japanese SMG**
**Rate of Fire: 450 rpm**
**Round Capacity: 30**
**Max Ammo: 500**
**Alt Fire: Rifle Butt Bash**
**Weight: 7.3 pounds**

**Description:** The Type 100 was the only submachine gun used by the Japanese during World War II. It was time-consuming and expensive to build. The Type 100 was not built in large numbers compared to most other nations, with less than 30,000 being completed by the war's end. It has a side mounted magazine and includes a bayonet mount.

**Gameplay Notes:** Like the Arisaka, the Type 100 is frequently used by Japanese soldiers. It has noticeably less recoil and muzzle flash than the Allied submachine guns. If you're fighting in short- or mid-range firefights, pick up this weapon (if it's available).

## Model 96 6.5mm Light Machine Gun (With Bayonet)

**Ammo Type: Japanese MG**
**Rate of Fire: 550 rpm**
**Round Capacity: 30**
**Max Ammo: 500**
**Alt Fire: Bayonet Stab**
**Weight: 20 pounds + magazine and bayonet**

**Description:** This is a gas-operated, magazine-fed, air-cooled, fully automatic light machine gun. It has a telescopic sight with a 10 degree field of view and a 2.5x zoom.

**Gameplay Notes:** The gun has a small bipod mounted toward the end of the barrel, which automatically extends when you use the weapon while prone. Heavier than the Johnson LMG, this gun prevents you from running quickly, but it has the added bonus of a sniper scope and a bayonet.

## Model 97 Grenade

**Ammo Type: Japanese Grenade**
**Delay: 5 seconds**

**Description:** Typical front-line infantry fragmentation grenade.

**Gameplay Notes:** This weapon operates just like the Allied Mark II grenade.

## MOUNTED

Mounted machine guns are harder to shoot in continuous bursts because of their large muzzle flashes as well as their tendency to cause the screen to shake increasingly as you hold the fire button. This makes it difficult to just hold down the trigger and mow down enemy after enemy. The most effective way to use mounted machine guns is in short bursts of 10 or so rounds. You also must reload mounted machine guns, and they have potentially limited ammo. When the machine gun runs out of ammo, it reloads automatically.

## Allied

### *Browning M2 .50 Caliber Water-Cooled MG*

**Rate of Fire: 500 rpm**
**Round Capacity: 200-round metallic-link belt and ammo chest**
**Max Ammo: Variable**
**Date entered into production: mid 1930s**

**Description:** Water-cooling prevented the weapon from overheating. Versatile weapon that could be used against airplanes and ground forces.

**Gameplay Notes:**
The Browning machine gun is the most common mounted weapon you see on the Allied side. Take any chance you get to use this weapon on large groups of enemies.

## 60mm M2 Portable Mortar

**Rate of Fire:** 30 rpm max
**Round Capacity:** 1
**Max Ammo:** Variable
**Weight:** 42 pounds
**Date entered into production:** 1940

**Description:** The 60mm M2 Mortar was developed in response to the need for a weapon effective between the ranges of hand grenades and the 81mm mortar. Like its 81mm cousin, the 60mm's operation was identical and the unit could be broken down into three basic units: barrel, bipod, and baseplate. These mortars could fire Heavy Explosive or Incendiary (white phosphorous) ammo, but our game will only have the former.

**Gameplay Notes:** The M2 cannot be fired until you press Alt Fire to place the weapon on the ground and set it up. Press the Aim key to bring up the targeting reticle. Adjust the pitch with the mouse, then press the Fire button to launch the mortar. Press Alt Fire again to pick up the weapon.

## Air-Cooled .50 Cal Mounted AA MG (West Virginia)

**Rate of Fire:** 500 rpm
**Round Capacity:** 200-round metallic-link belt and ammo chest
**Max Ammo:** Infinite

**Description:** Air-cooling prevented the weapon from overheating. Versatile weapon that could be used against airplanes and ground forces.

**Gameplay Notes:** This weapon is easy to aim quickly and has a high rate of fire but lacks the direct firepower of the larger AA guns.

## 1.1 inch Quad-Mounted AA Gun (West Virginia)

**Rate of Fire:** 500 rpm
**Round Capacity:** 200-round
metallic-link belt and ammo chest
**Max Ammo:** Infinite

**Description:** An unreliable weapon, the 1.1 inch quads were one of the earlier anti-air weapons that were quickly replaced after Pearl Harbor.

**Gameplay Notes:** The Quad AA gun has a slow rate of fire and poor accuracy but excellent firepower. You can take down an enemy plane with one direct hit.

> **NOTE:** You find both of these AA guns only on the *West Virginia* during the Pearl Harbor mission.

## 40mm Bofor AA Gun

**Rate of Fire:** 120 rpm
**Round Capacity:** 1
**Max Ammo:** Infinite

**Description:** It was used to defend airfields and other military establishments against low-level enemy attack. It fired a 2 lbs (1 kg) high explosive shell at 2800 ft/sec (848 m/sec) at 120 rounds per minute. The Bofor's maximum ceiling was 7151 meters but the most effective ceiling was 3787 meters.

**Gameplay Notes:** The Bofor is a high-powered AA gun. However, the rate of fire is low, so you need to lead your target by a considerable amount to score a hit. Use this weapon to shoot down enemy fighter planes during the Henderson Field mission.

## Japanese

## Model 92 Heavy Machine Gun

**Rate of Fire: 450 rpm**
**Round Capacity: 30-round strips**
**Max Ammo: Variable**

**Description:** This is the standard Japanese heavy machine gun. It is gas-operated, strip-fed, fully automatic, and air-cooled. A semi-automatic heavy gun. It has a violent recoil and can cause a ton of damage. Armor-piercing tracer and high-explosive tracer ammo types can be used.

**Gameplay Notes:** The Model 92 operates just like the Browning M2. Because you spend most of your time behind enemy lines, the Model 92 is the most common mounted weapon you encounter in the campaign.

## Model 96 25mm AA/AT Triple Mount Cannon

**Rate of Fire: 300 rpm**
**Round Capacity: 15**
**Max Ammo: Infinite**

**Description:** The standard Japanese mobile heavy anti-aircraft weapon. This is a truck-drawn weapon. When firing, the wheels are removed and the gun is supported by five outriggers. It can also be used against ground targets. It can use high explosive, shrapnel, or incendiary ammo.

**Gameplay Notes:** The Tri-Mount cannon is another high-powered AA gun. However, you can also use it against targets on the ground if they are within the gun's sights. Usually, the gun is pointed away from the field, making it difficult to use.

## GROUND

### Type 95 Scout Car

#### History

The Type 95 was a lightweight 4x4 reconnaissance vehicle that was developed after the Manchurian incident demonstrated to the Japanese Army the need for such a vehicle. The Type 95 was built by Kurogane and was the Japanese army's only entirely natively designed vehicle of its type. Most of the others were derived from American designs. This car was first manufactured in 1937 and was the most widely used machine of its type by Japanese forces on all fronts during World War II.

#### Gameplay

You use this jeep in Makin Atoll to break into the fuel depot, and again in Tarawa to escape Red Beach 2. You can't actually control the jeep; your teammates drive while you hang on for dear life. The Type 95 has 1000 "life" points, but it takes very little damage in both of the missions where you ride inside. You needn't worry about the enemy destroying it.

## SEA

### Elco PT-20 Class Boat

### History

The Elco boats were the largest in size of the three types of PT Boats built for United States Navy use during World War II. The primary mission of the PT Boat was to attack surface ships and craft. PTs were also used effectively to lay mines and smoke screens, to rescue downed aviators, and to carry out intelligence or raider operations.

### Gameplay

You man one of these boats during the Pearl Harbor mission. The boat's armament includes a machine gun you use to shoot down the enemy planes while en route to the USS *West Virginia*.

## AIR

### Grumman F4F Wildcat

#### History

This stubby but rugged plane was the main fighter for the U.S. Navy and Marines during the hard-fought first year of the war. While not as fast or as agile as its opponent, the Japanese Zero, superior training and tactics of its pilots allowed it to win many aerial combats.

#### Gameplay

This plane is the only vehicle that you get to pilot on your own (in the Flyboys mission). The Strafe keys and mouse control the plane's movement and the Move Forward key accelerates it. The plane has 1000 "life" points, so you must dodge enemy fire whenever possible while flying it. The Wildcat has a gun on the front as well as the back (you switch between them over the course of the mission).

### PBY Catalina Black Cat

#### History

The PBY Catalina "Black Cats" were Navy Catalina Patrol seaplanes or "flying boats." They were painted black for night bombing operations against Japanese shipping in the Southwest Pacific. In the daytime, they flew air-sea rescue missions—picking up ditched aircrews and pilots from the Army bomber and fighter strikes.

#### Gameplay

The last objective of the Henderson mission has you protecting one of these transport planes from enemy fighters. It's a much larger plane than the other enemy (and friendly) planes, so it's easy to spot.

## Mitsubishi A6M "Zero"

### History

The Mitsubishi A6M was the most famous Japanese plane of World War II. The "Zero" was armed with two 20mm cannons and two 7.7mm machine guns and it possessed the incredible range of 1930 miles using a centerline drop tank. Though outclassed by more powerful U.S. fighters after late 1943, the Zero remained a tough opponent throughout the war.

### Gameplay

This is the most common enemy plane you see throughout the game. You shoot them down with AA Guns in Pearl Harbor and Guadalcanal and blow them out of the sky during the Flyboys mission.

# PEARL HARBOR

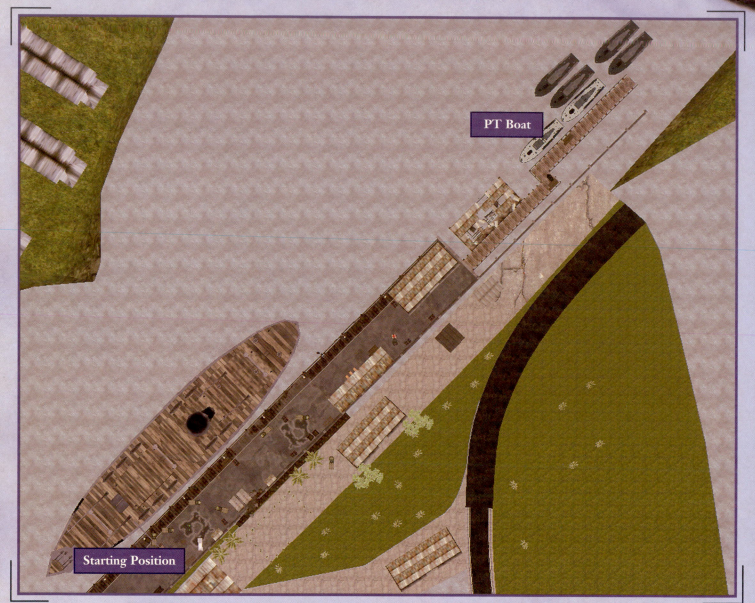

PT Boat

Starting Position

## Briefing

### Mission Objectives

- **Get to the PT Boat Alive**
- **Find Counter-Flood Valve**
- **Get Topside and Defend the** *West Virginia*
- **Use 50-cal Gun to Protect the** *Nevada*
- **Use Quad AA Gun to Protect the** *West Virginia*

### Available Weapons
**None**

## MISSION: WALKTHROUGH

### Objective: Get to the PT Boat Alive

Once you gain control of your character, immediately take cover. Head northeast and stay behind cover as much as possible. If you take any significant damage, find a safe spot and call a medic.

When you reach the end of the pier, hop on the boat to the left. You hear a command to man the guns, but before you can help, a stray shot knocks you out. When you come to, man the gun and take down the enemy planes. When you reach the ship, you climb into the lower level on your own.

TIP: AIM AT THE CLOSEST PLANES, BECAUSE THE DISTANT TARGETS ARE TOO FAR AWAY TO HIT ACCURATELY.

## Objective: Find Counter-Flood Valve

Crawl through the hole to the right and move to the closed door. Wait for the wall to blow open and then slowly walk through the hole the explosion created. If you try to run right through the room, the steam from the broken boiler will scald you. Check the near side of the boiler for a steam valve. Hold the Use key to turn the valve and shut off the steam. Then, head to the ladder at the far right corner.

At the top of the platform, find the valves on the right. Shut off both valves, then cross the catwalk to the platform on the opposite end. Shut off the valve there, then climb back onto the catwalk and walk through the doorway at the end.

Climb down the ladder on the right at the catwalk's far end. Wait for an explosion at the other side of the room, then wade through the water to that side and find the valve against the wall. Turn the wheel all the way, then turn to your right and find the counter-flood valve. Press and hold the Use key to use the valve and complete the objective.

## Objective: Get Topside and Defend the West Virginia

Backtrack to the ladder and proceed through the door on the right. Follow the sailor to the ladder on the right and climb up to the next level. Keep following and run through the hall as quickly as possible. When you reach the open room, find the axe on the far wall. Use the axe on the gas canister on the floor. The canister ruptures and slides across the room, blowing open the jammed door.

Walk into the next room and look for the injured sailor on the ground (he has an exclamation point above his head). Press the Use key to pick him up and carry him to the medic.

> **TIP: IF YOU'RE INJURED, TAKE ADVANTAGE OF THE MEDIC FOR YOURSELF, TOO.**

Head into the hall on the right and go prone to avoid the fire. Use your axe to crack the pipe on the left and stop the fire stream. Proceed through the door and find another injured sailor on the room's left side. Bring him back to the medic, then head to the door on the right and hit it repeatedly with your axe to open it. Walk around the fire on the right and use your axe to destroy the crates. Climb the ladder to reach the upper level.

Proceed through the open doors and look for injured sailors. Find the first one trapped under some ammo boxes. Use your axe to clear away the boxes, then pick him up and carry him to the medic at the end of the hall (near the stairs). The XO is also injured, and trapped behind a jammed door. Use your axe to open the door and then carry the XO to the medic. Climb the stairs and use your axe to clear away the debris and reach the deck.

## Objective: Use 50-cal Gun to Protect the *Nevada*

Run around to the opposite side of the deck and look for the AA guns. Climb the stairs and man the first small AA gun on the left. As before, aim at the closest planes to do the most good. When the *Nevada* is clear, hop off the 50-cal and head to the Quad AA gun.

## Objective: Use Quad AA Gun to Protect the *West Virginia*

Listen for your spotter's directions to decide where to aim. As usual, aim for the closest planes, especially the ones flying straight toward your position. Once you've blown enough planes out of the sky, you complete the level.

# Makin Atoll

## MISSION: NIGHT MOVES

Starting Position

To Map 2

## Briefing

### Mission Objectives

- **Destroy AA Gun Emplacement**
- **Destroy Japanese Radio Tower**

## Available Weapons

- **.45 Magnum**
- **Springfield M1903**
- **Nambu**
- **Arisaka**

Map 3 Start

Camp 1

Radio Tower

Camp 2

## Objective: Destroy AA Gun Emplacement

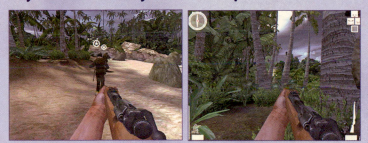

Follow your squad to the first checkpoint and eliminate the first group of Japanese soldiers. Continue along the path until more soldiers attack from behind the trees. Stay with your squad and take down all the enemy soldiers. Scan the platforms in the trees for snipers.

When you reach the camp, wait for your orders, then creep around to the left and hide behind the crates. When the gunfire begins, start shooting. Take down any soldiers directly behind the crates, then back up to get a better view of the area. If you spend too much time in one spot, a soldier will rush you and do serious damage with his bayonet. After you've killed all the enemy soldiers, set an explosive charge on the AA Gun and then regroup with your squad.

## Objective: Destroy Japanese Radio Tower

Meet your squad at the edge of the water. When everyone is in position, start shooting the soldiers on the bridge across the water. Then, move through the water and finish off the other soldiers in the area.

Follow your squad along the path to the next camp. When you reach the middle of the camp area, more soldiers attack from inside the huts. Shoot through the windows to deal with them, then move to the next camp.

**TIP: Check inside the huts for ammo.**

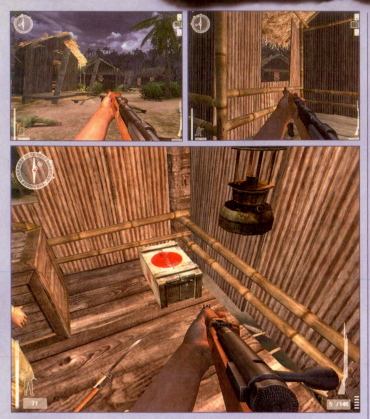

Follow your men to the Radio Tower site. Set the charge to complete the objective.

More soldiers are here, hidden just like before. Plug every soldier you can see, then move around the side of the huts to advance on the enemy's position. As you reach the far end of the camp, more soldiers appear. Drop this new group, then check the rest of the huts for any stragglers (and ammo).

## MISSION: MAN DOWN

Starting Position

Enemy Camp

To Map 2

## Briefing

### *Mission Objectives*

- **Destroy the Island Fuel Depot**
- **Rescue Pilot**

### *Available Weapons*

- **.45 Magnum**
- **Reising SMG**
- **Nambu**
- **Arisaka**
- **Model 100 SMG**

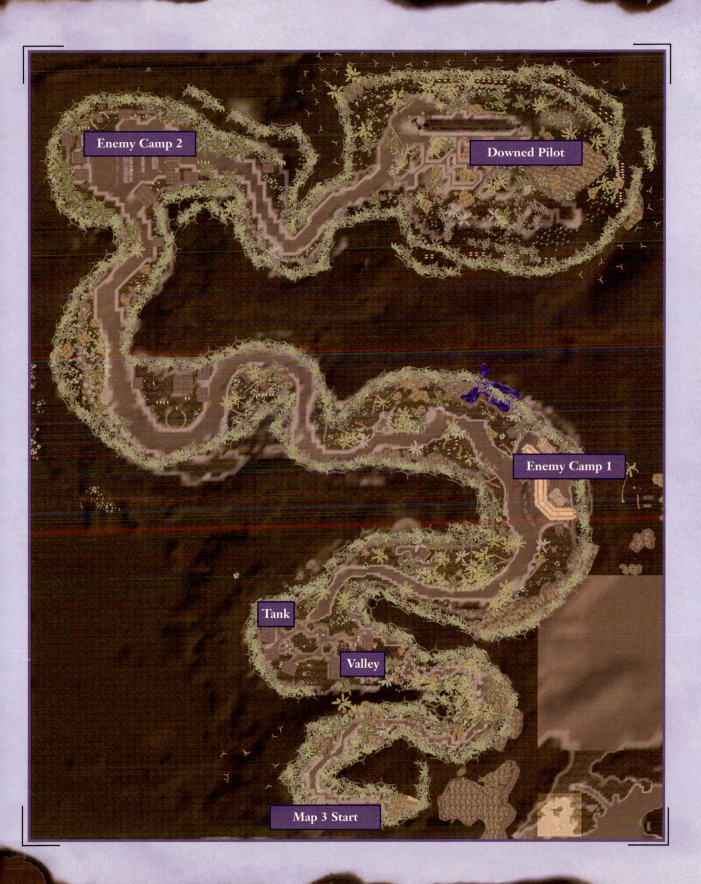

## Objective: Destroy the Island Fuel Depot

Crawl through the underbrush until you reach the road, then follow the road to the left. Once the enemy discovers you, gun down the soldiers, then regroup and continue along the road. Dispose of the soldiers hiding behind the trees on the right of the road, then move up. Prepare for a jeep full of soldiers to drive up behind you.

> **TIP: PICK UP ONE OF THE JAPANESE ARISAKA RIFLES. IT WILL SERVE YOU MUCH BETTER THAN THE REISING SUBMACHINE GUN.**

Get back onto the road and keep walking. Eliminate the soldiers behind the cover to the left and the brush on the right. Keep to the bushes and advance toward your objective (follow your compass).

When you see a truck in the distance, get ready for more shooting. Gun down the soldiers who drop out of the truck, then move past the truck and keep following the road. Continue through the brush to find an emplaced machine gun. Nail the soldier manning the gun, then take his place and use the machine gun to destroy the tank that drives up on the right.

Get back on the road and keep at it. More soldiers run in from the distance. Take them down and then proceed. Look for a tower in the camp ahead. Shoot the sniper in the tower, then deal with the group of soldiers that attack from the right. When the coast is clear, advance into the camp.

Eliminate the soldiers in the closest buildings, then creep around to the left to flank the rest. When the area is secure, check the buildings for ammo, then continue following your compass. Clear out the remaining soldiers on the road and keep going.

There's another camp at the end of the path. Approach slowly, then take cover and deal with the soldiers in the buildings on the left and hiding at the far end of the camp. Then, check the huts for ammo and find the path on the right (near the shore) to continue.

Head into the brush on the left and stay low. When you see the enemy camp, take your time and aim to take out one soldier. This is the only chance you'll get before all hell breaks loose. When the enemy soldiers are all down, proceed through the camp to the path on the right.

This path leads to yet another camp full of soldiers, so get ready. Take out the sniper in the tower first, then stay low and gun down the other soldiers that run onto the path. Once the coast is clear, proceed through the camp to the next path. Walk to the end of the path and eliminate the guards in the clearing. Watch out for the shooters in the buildings on the left. Then, find the jeep on the west side of the camp to continue.

Now, it's time for a wild ride. As the jeep drives, pick off any soldiers you can. Once you reach the fuel depot and jump off the jeep, hide immediately behind the cover on the right and nail the soldiers in the area.

> **TIP:** Mow down enemy soldiers with the machine gun.

When you've eliminated any soldiers you can see from behind the machine gun, scour the area for any survivors and finish them off. Then, place an explosive charge on the large fuel tank near the fence. Regroup with your squad to get your new orders and move out.

## Objective: Rescue Pilot

Follow your men along the path. When the gunfire begins, stay covered and meet your squad near the small clearing in the brush. Aim down into the valley and pick off any soldiers you see. Nail the enemy gunner in the perch as well.

> **WARNING:** Don't stick your head out too far or you risk taking damage from the tank.

Continue on the path and look for more targets. When you reach the valley, take cover behind the shack. You can't destroy the tank from here; you must set an explosive charge on the back of it.

Creep along the left side of the camp, using the crates as cover to finish off the rest of the soldiers. When you reach the end of the camp, walk around to the back of the tank and set the charge. Then, find the path on the right side of the camp and continue. Stay in the brush and nail the soldiers hiding in the next camp.

Crawl through the brush and take cover behind the trees. When you've cleared the immediate area, switch to the right side of the camp and move up to deal with more targets. When all the soldiers are down, follow your squad further into the camp to take on more enemies.

> **TIP: USE THE MACHINE GUN TO MAKE SHORT WORK OF THE SOLDIERS.**

Follow the path to the next camp and use the rocks on the left as cover. There are many enemy soldiers here, so stay covered until all the shooting stops. Check the area for ammo, then get back on the path and keep going. Get comfortable behind cover and take out the soldiers in the next camp. Pick off the shooters in the perches and shoot the barrels to do some quick damage to any enemies hiding near them.

Follow your squad along the path and into another clearing to find the downed pilot. Quickly pick up the pilot and carry him back toward the entrance to the clearing. Several enemy

soldiers rush into the area, so put the pilot down behind a rock and take up a defensive position. When you've dispatched all the soldiers, pick up the pilot again and carry him onto the path.

## MISSION: SITTING DUCKS

Starting Position

Rafts

Mortar 1

Mortar 3

Mortar 2

Willy

## Briefing

### Mission Objectives
- Hold Off Attacking Force
- Eliminate Mortar Crews
- Find Willy

## Available Weapons

- .45 Magnum
- Reising SMG
- Springfield M1903
- Nambu
- Arisaka
- Model 100 SMG

## Objective: Hold Off Attacking Force

As soon as the intro finishes, soldiers immediately attack you from behind. Run to the right and take cover behind the large rock in the water. Help your men eliminate all of the enemy soldiers and then follow the squad into the jungle.

## Objective: Eliminate Mortar Crews

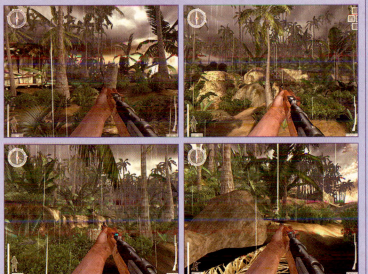

Hide behind trees and take on the advancing soldiers. Look for the first mortar in the distance beyond the hut. Pick off the soldier manning the mortar, then finish off the remaining soldiers. The second mortar is on the same ridge as the first, but farther to the right of the hut. Finally, the third mortar is close to the beach, hidden in the brush to the far right. Check the hut for ammo, then head back to the beach.

## Objective: Find Willy

Head back into the jungle to search for Willy. Creep along the rocks on the left and hide in the brush. You have a chance to take down one enemy soldier before the rest see you, so make your shot count. When you've cleared out the soldiers, follow your compass to find Willy behind a log (he has an exclamation point above his head). Pick up Willy and carry him to the raft to finish the level.

# GUADALCANAL
## MISSION: Henderson

## Briefing

### Mission Objectives

- Rally Up with Marines at Henderson Air Field
- Secure Enemy Artillery Position
- Return to Henderson
- Clear the Camp of Enemies
- Help Friendly Fighters Get Airborne
- Reclaim West AA Guns
- Shoot Down Zeros Chasing the Black Cat

## Available Weapons

- Colt .45

- Thompson SMG

- M1 Carbine

- Arisaka

To Map 3

Enemy Camp

Artillery

Trench

Hidden Path

Start Map 2

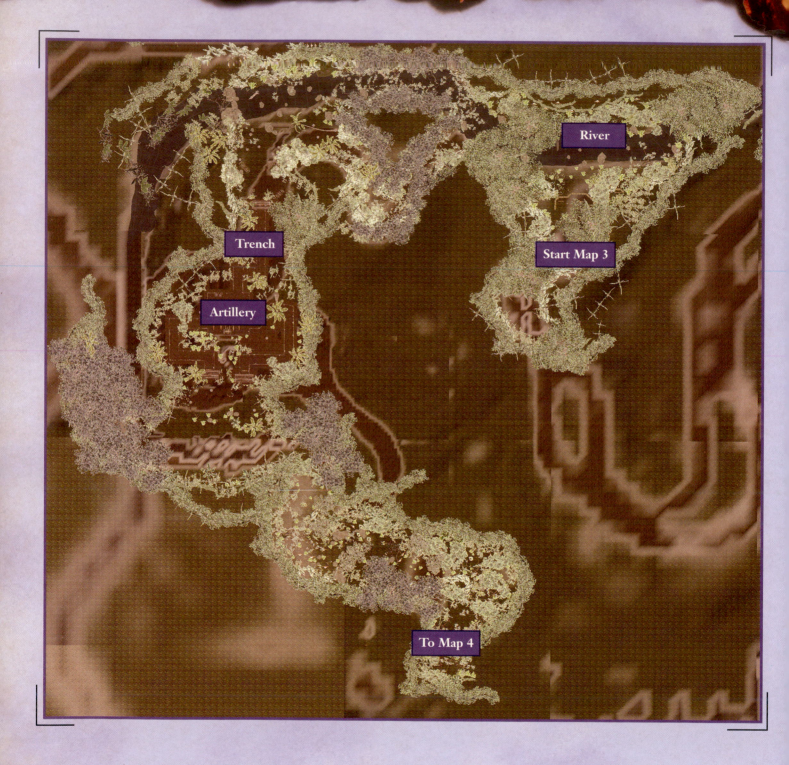

River

Trench

Start Map 3

Artillery

To Map 4

Start Map 4

Campsite

West AA Guns

AA Gun 1

Runway

Hangars

## Objective: Rally Up with Marines at Henderson Air Field

Follow your squad until you reach the edge of the enemy village. When the gunfire starts, seek cover and move around to the left of the village. Several enemy soldiers advance on your position, but they show up one at a time, so you can take them down easily.

Move farther into the village and pick off the soldiers who run out of the hut on the right. Advance onto the balcony of the hut and drop the soldiers manning the machine gun. Then, deal with the remaining soldiers hiding at the village's far end.

Continue around to the left of the village to find a path leading to more huts. Take cover behind the trees and eliminate the soldiers hiding in the huts.

> **TIP:** WHEN ALL THE SOLDIERS ARE DISPOSED OF, CHECK THE HUTS FOR AMMO AND A MAP THAT WILL AID YOU LATER.

Rally up with your teammates, then follow your squad along the path to find the airfield. When the bombs start dropping, hop on the truck and enjoy the ride...

## Objective: Secure Enemy Artillery Position

After your little "accident" on the truck, you wake up on a side path. Follow your squad to the edge of the enemy camp. Nail the soldier manning the machine gun, then creep up the hill and pick off the other soldier hiding behind the wall.

Climb up over the wall and down into the trench. Creep through the trench until you reach a turnoff to the right. Peek around the corner and plug the closest waiting soldier. Then, back up and wait for more soldiers to rush you. Gun them all down, then head into the clearing where the soldiers were waiting.

> **WARNING:** While waiting for the soldiers to run at you, watch out for grenades. Back up if you see one fly in.

Take the path on the right and meet up with your squad mates. Gun down all the soldiers who jump over the wall and attack. When you've disposed of all of them, return to the clearing and set an explosive charge to destroy the artillery cannon.

## Objective: Return to Henderson

Walk through the new hole in the side of the trench and stick with your squad. When you reach the edge of the enemy encampment, scan the buildings for targets. Once you've dealt with the immediate threat, push into the camp and finish off the survivors. Find the path at the end of the camp and continue.

As you move into the trees, the enemy will ambush you. Back up and take cover near the camp to take all the soldiers down. Keep following the path and watch for more soldiers in the distance.

Follow your squad to the edge of the river. When the enemy soldiers advance on your position, take cover behind the sandbags and gun them all down. When you've dealt with all of the soldiers, head down into the river and rally up. Follow the river to the first clearing, then take cover and get ready for a big fight.

Start by eliminating the soldiers who rush you from the right side of the river. Then, pick off the other soldiers who advance from the far left side. When the large force runs at you, back up quite a bit along the river and take cover. From here, it's much easier to gun down the enemy as they slowly wade through the water.

> **TIP:** If you see a grenade fly toward your position, back up and take cover until it explodes.

Once you've finally disposed of all the enemy troops, continue up the river and walk up onto the bank (follow your compass). Nail the soldier manning the machine gun, then walk up over the wall and into the trench. Round the corner and pick off the soldiers near the artillery gun.

When the tanks approach, get on the artillery and take 'em down. When the coast is clear, move down into the valley and follow the path to the left. More enemies are hiding in the bushes here, so stay covered and eliminate them all. Then, keep following your compass through the brush.

## Objective: Clear the Camp of Enemies

Follow the path until you reach the campsite. As soon as you enter the camp, enemy soldiers run in and attack. Take cover behind the buildings to dispose of them. When you reach the machine gun, quickly take up position behind it and gun down the soldiers who charge your position. When you've secured the area, walk to the small building next to the jeep and head through it to reach the airfield.

Start by picking off the enemies in the corner across the field. When that area is clear, move around the corner to the right and take down the soldiers who charge across the runway.

**TIP:** Before the soldiers run across the runway, quickly hop on the AA Gun to the right of the trench and gun down the enemy. Sure, it's cruel, but it works.

## Objective: Help Friendly Fighters Get Airborne

Get on the AA gun and shoot down the enemy planes. Once all of your friendly planes have taken off, you're good to go.

**NOTE:** Enemy planes all have red circles on the bottom of their wings.

## Objective: Reclaim West AA Guns

Walk along the runway to the right. Eliminate the soldiers who run over the hills and the others near the building in the distance. Use the building as cover and clear the entire area of enemies.

**WARNING:** In this area, fighters frequently fly low and fire on your position. Don't stay in one spot for too long.

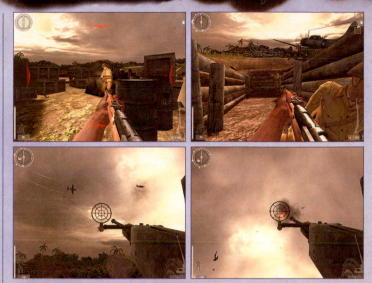

Keep moving west, dropping any enemy soldiers who get in your way. When you reach the AA Gun, hop on and protect the hangars from the enemy planes. The divebombers fly in from the southwest, so aim up to the right of the hangars and take down the planes before they drop the bombs.

## Objective: Shoot Down Zeros Chasing the Black Cat

Don't dismount that AA Gun just yet, soldier; there're more bogies to shoot down. Look for the Black Cat in the sky (it's a large black airplane) and aim for the planes chasing it. You need to lead the enemy planes to hit them, so aim at the Black Cat's tail.

## MISSION: BLOODY RIDGE

To Map 2

Hidden Path

Second Ridge

Starting Position

First Ridge

### Briefing

*Mission Objectives*
- **Defend the First Ridge**
- **Clear the Jungle of Flanking Forces**
- **Defend the Third Ridge**

*Available Weapons*

- **Colt .45**

- **Nambu**

- **Model 100 SMG**

- **Garand**

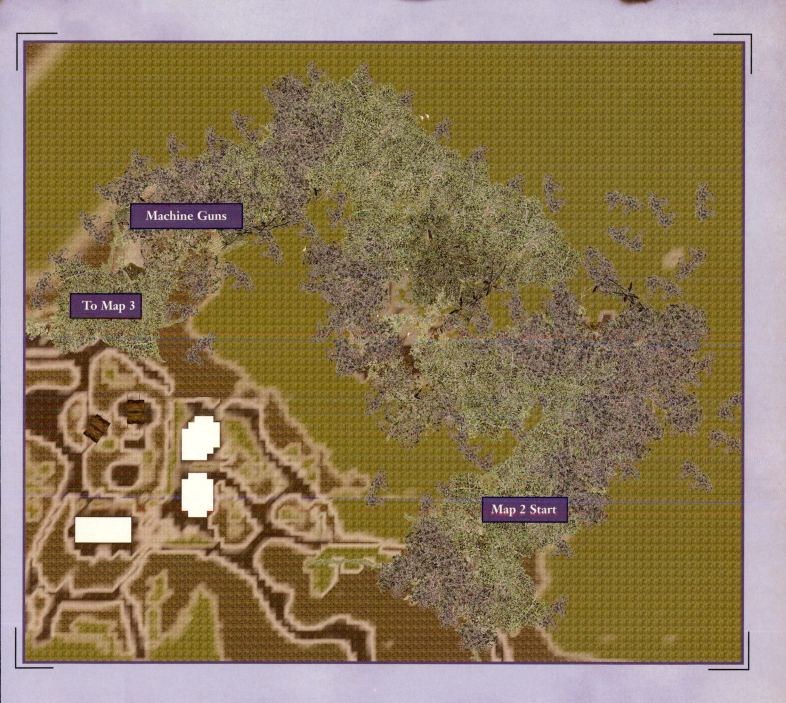

Machine Guns

To Map 3

Map 2 Start

## Objective: Defend the First Ridge

Mount the machine gun and listen for the direction to aim. You have limited ammo, so don't just hold the trigger; fire in short bursts at the closest soldiers. When the machine gun runs out of ammo, back up and take cover. Take down the remaining enemies with your rifle and then follow your squad into the jungle.

Head farther southeast into the jungle to find a hidden friendly position where you get free health and ammo and a bonus area that skips the defense of the second ridge.

## Objective: Clear the Jungle of Flanking Forces

Slowly creep along the path until you hear enemy soldiers advancing. Back up and take cover in the trees to eliminate the soldiers. When the area is clear, continue down the path, dropping all the soldiers who attack. When you reach the end of the path, friendly forces help you finish off the enemies. Walk a little farther up the path and climb over the rock to reach the third ridge.

## Objective: Defend the Third Ridge

Move up the hill to the Allied camp and take up position at the open machine gun. Mow down the soldiers until you see one of your men (carrying ammo) take a bullet. Dismount the machine gun and head to his position. Pick up the ammo box and carry it down the hill to the friendly soldiers manning the machine gun. Drop off the ammo, then walk back up the hill, pick up the injured soldier, and carry him to the medic tent.

Get back on the machine gun and keep attacking the enemies. When your gun runs out of ammo, head around to the right and mount another gun to deal with the soldiers who attack from the right. After enough enemy soldiers go down, you complete the objective.

## MISSION: RIVER WALK

Starting Position

Right Fork

Portable
Machine Gun

Ridge

Valley

To Map 2

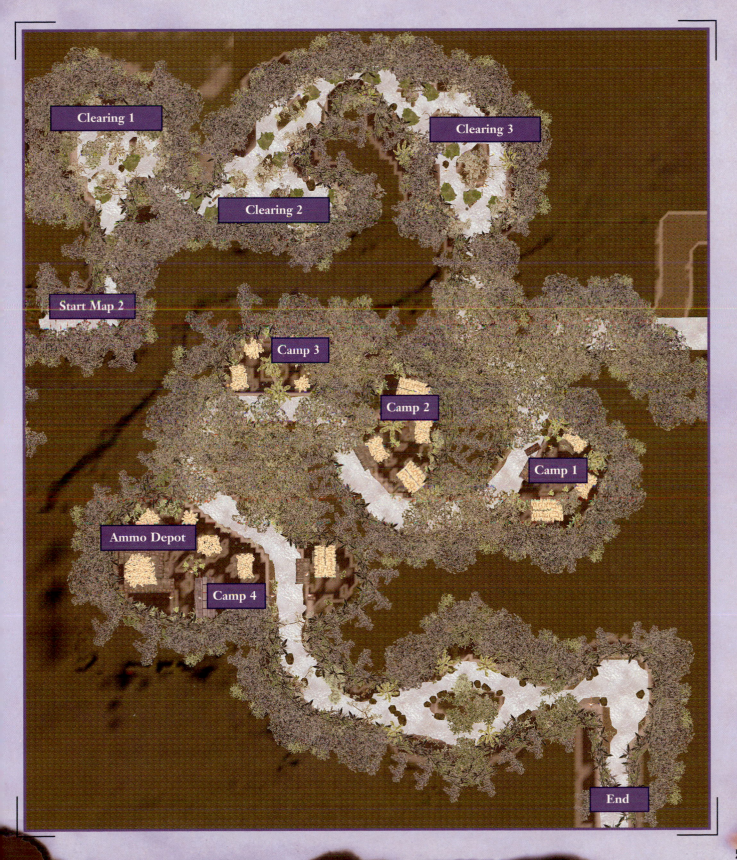

- Clearing 1
- Clearing 3
- Clearing 2
- Start Map 2
- Camp 3
- Camp 2
- Camp 1
- Ammo Depot
- Camp 4
- End

## Briefing

### Mission Objectives

- Scout the Right Fork of the River
- Eliminate Japanese River Patrols
- Traverse through the Swamp
- Clear Japanese River Camps
- Destroy the Ammo Depot
- Eliminate Remaining Japanese Patrols

### Available Weapons

- Colt .45

- Thompson SMG

- Arisaka

- Model 100 SMG

## Objective: Scout the Right Fork of the River

> NOTE: Your only weapon at the beginning of this area is your Colt .45.

Follow your teammate through the river and into the brush. When you reach the ridge, take cover behind the rocks and use your binoculars to peer into the valley below. When you glimpse the soldiers, head back toward the river.

Keep following your teammate to reach the small enemy camp. Go prone and sneak through the brush to the machine gun. Quickly mount the gun and mow down the enemy soldiers. When you've dropped them all, press Alt Fire to pick up the machine gun and carry it with you. Then, return to your squad.

Gun down the enemy patrols as they enter the area. When your men move up, pick up the machine gun and follow them. Keep blasting the patrols as you follow the river. When the portable machine gun runs out of ammo, leave it behind (carrying it just slows you down). When you reach the end of the river and climb over the waterfall, you complete the objective.

> **TIP:** TAKE THE OPPORTUNITY BETWEEN PATROLS TO RELOAD THE MACHINE GUN.

## Objective: Eliminate Japanese River Patrols

Head downriver with your men, then stop and set up the portable machine gun when they stop to take cover.

## Objective: Traverse through the Swamp

Crawl along the left side of the swamp until you reach the clearing with the large trees. Hide in the brush on the left as enemy soldiers attack. Use the rocks and trees as cover to take down the enemy.

Continue following your squad through the swamp. When you reach the next clearing, more soldiers attack. Eliminate them as before, then keep going. Eventually, you reach a small waterfall that plunges into a lower part of the swamp. Aim over the edge and plug the waiting enemy soldiers, walk over the waterfall, and proceed.

## Objective: Clear Japanese River Camps

The first river camp is just ahead. Move up and aim at the soldier in the closest sniper tower. Take your time to aim, plug him, then back up and take cover (now that the enemy has spotted you). Stay covered and nail all the soldiers in the camp. When the camp is secure, follow the river through the camp and back into the brush.

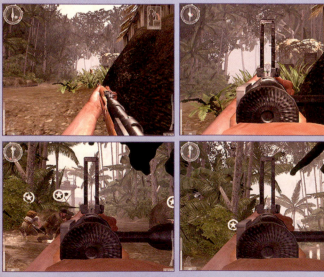

As soon as you reach the rocks, more soldiers attack. Use the rocks as cover and gun down the opposition. Clear out

the camp on the right and then head through to the right to find another camp. Clear out all the soldiers, then move into the camp. You can see into the next river camp from this one, so use the huts as cover and shoot the advancing enemies.

## Objective: Destroy the Ammo Depot

When you've completely cleared out the camp, find the ammo boxes on the right and set an explosive charge to destroy them.

## Objective: Eliminate Remaining Japanese Patrols

Follow the river through the camp to the clearing and hide behind the rocks. Aim up into the trees and nail the snipers, then continue along the river to complete the objective.

## MISSION: VILLAGE

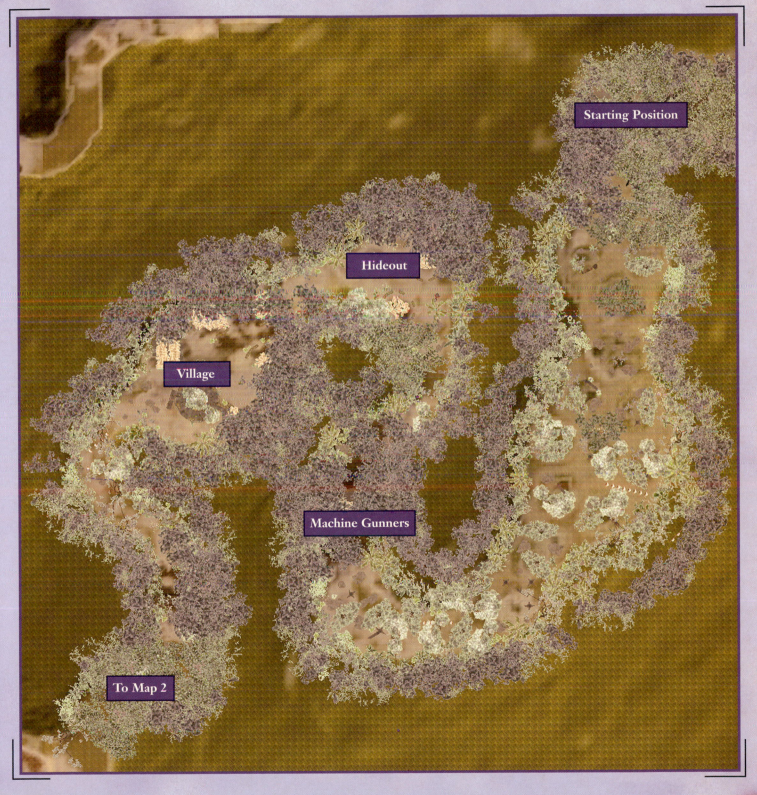

Starting Position

Hideout

Village

Machine Gunners

To Map 2

Bridge

To Map 3

Village 4

Village 3

Start Map 2

Village 2

Hidden Path

POWs

Village 1

Artillery Installment

Beach

Trench 2

Trench 1

Start Map 3

## Briefing

### Mission Objectives

- Infiltrate the Village
- Secure the Village
- Clear Jungle Valley of Japanese Forces
- Clean Out Japanese Trench System
- Breach the Artillery Defenses
- Destroy the Artillery Installment

### Available Weapons

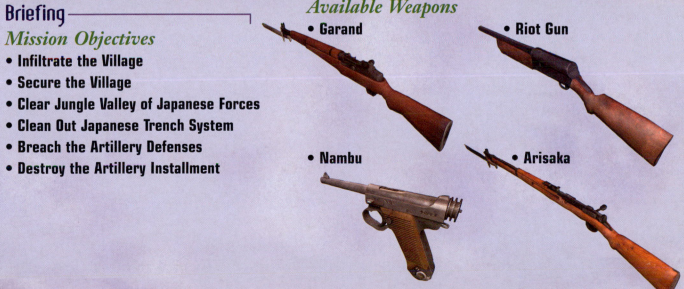

- Garand
- Riot Gun
- Nambu
- Arisaka

## Objective: Infiltrate the Village

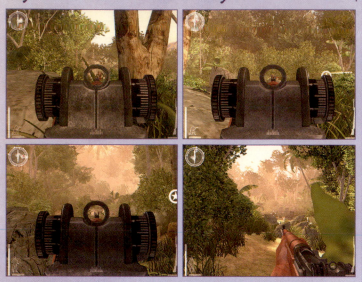

Move forward and use the rocks as cover as the enemy attacks. Quickly plug all the soldiers before they charge. Then, follow your men to the edge of the trees ahead and gun down the next attacking force. Keep following your squad and clearing out the enemy until you reach the bend in the path. Pop the two soldiers manning the machine guns, then move up to the bunker and climb over. Follow the path to the edge of the village and eliminate the soldiers hiding behind the crates.

## Objective: Secure the Village

Creep along the path toward the next section of the village. There are plenty of enemy soldiers to shoot in here, so get comfortable. If you can't see any more from your current position, walk along the area's left edge and flank the enemy. When the area is secure, get back on the path and continue.

> **TIP:** Check the huts throughout the village for ammo.

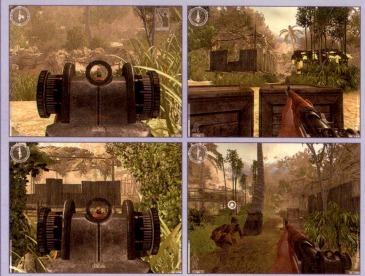

Proceed carefully through the brush—a disguised enemy hideout ahead is hard to see. When the soldiers run out, take them all down. Pass the hideout and stick with your squad. Around the next corner, you see another piece of the village. There are more enemies here, so do your job and gun them down. Move around to the right side of the camp and finish off the rest of the soldiers.

> **NOTE:** A hidden path on the left side of the village leads to a small enemy camp. You can rescue Allied prisoners of war here.

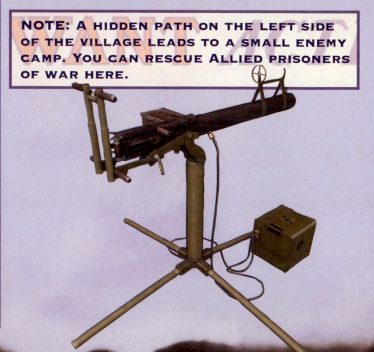

## Objective: Clear Jungle Valley of Japanese Forces

Creep through the brush along the side of the jungle path. Your first targets conveniently run right at you, but the others are a bit craftier. Watch the ridges on the sides of the path for hidden snipers as you proceed. The clearing at the end of the path is full of more soldiers, so hide behind the trees and eliminate them. After the plane bombs the bridge, continue forward and get back on the path.

> **TIP:** To protect the Allied plane, simply shoot any soldier who climbs into the tower on the left of the bridge.

Stick to the path's right wall and nail the snipers on the ridge to the left. When you reach the edge of the clearing, stay covered as much as possible. Cap the soldiers in the towers and in the brush on the right side of the camp.

## Objective: Clean Out Japanese Trench System

> **NOTE:** A hidden objective is to destroy all enemy towers. Before you leave a camp, find the red icon on the leg of each tower and set an explosive charge.

Climb down into the trench and take the middle path. The corners of the trench walls make great cover. Carefully proceed through the trench, using the corners as cover whenever the enemy attacks. When you've cleared out the trench, climb out at the right side and take the path out of the camp.

Enemy soldiers are hiding behind the rocks on the beach. Take advantage of the rocks near the edge of the path to plug each soldier from a safe position. When the area is clear, follow the beach to the left and find the next camp. Take down all the soldiers behind the rocks and in the towers.

> **TIP:** If you can reach the other end of the camp, climb into the tower and use the enemy's machine gun against them.

## Objective: Breach the Artillery Defenses

Follow the path at the back end of the camp until you reach the next clearing. Slowly move around the right side of the camp. Watch for enemy soldiers on the ledges to the left.

## Objective: Destroy the Artillery Installment

When you reach the end of the path around the camp, find the entrance down into the artillery installment and stop at the corner. There are enemy soldiers in the tunnel on the left and you're on your own down here. Look around the corner and plug any targets you see. If you see them throw a grenade your way, back around the corner and wait for it to explode. When it's clear, head through the tunnel to the first clearing.

There are more soldiers through the next tunnel, so creep forward and dispose of them just as you did the last group. Walk down into the last tunnel and cap the one remaining soldier. Then, find the red icon and set an explosive charge to complete the objective.

## MISSION: FLYBOYS

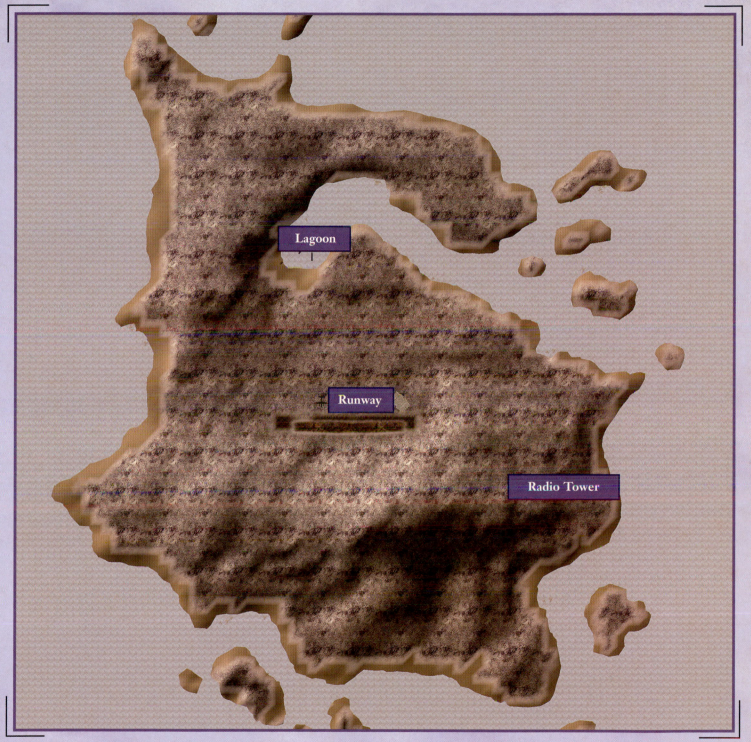

Lagoon

Runway

Radio Tower

## Briefing

### Mission Objectives

- **Fight Off Bandits**
- **Dogfight Bandits**
- **Destroy Radio Tower**
- **Destroy Lagoon Targets**
- **Eliminate Japanese Carrier and Japanese Destroyer**
- **Land Safely Aboard the USS** *Independence*

### Available Weapons

- **None**

## Objective: Fight Off Bandits

> **NOTE:** THIS MISSION TAKES PLACE ENTIRELY IN THE AIR.

The bandits are easy to spot, but be careful not to shoot your own plane while attacking them. The red dots on your radar indicate the bandits' positions. The larger the red dot, the closer the plane is. Aim for the closest planes to increase your accuracy.

Unlike the planes in the previous missions, these bandits take several hits to destroy. Keep on each plane until it goes down in flames. When you've destroyed all the bandits, press Use to climb into your plane's cockpit.

## Objective: Dogfight Bandits

This fight is basically like the previous one, but now you can actually control your plane. Use your radar to locate and pursue the enemy planes. Once you've shot them all down, use your radar to locate the Allied planes and fly to their location.

> **NOTE:** BOTH THE STRAFE KEYS AND MOUSE CONTROL THE PLANE. THE MOVE FORWARD KEY CAUSES THE PLANE TO ACCELERATE.

## Objective: Destroy Radio Tower

The radio tower shows up as a red box on your radar. Fly toward it, but also watch out for more enemy planes. After you destroy the radio tower, take out the enemy planes on the runway.

> **WARNING: DON'T FLY TOO LOW. IF YOU HIT THE GROUND, IT'S LIGHTS OUT FOR YOU.**

## Objective: Destroy Lagoon Targets

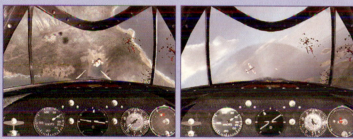

The targets you need to destroy are in the lagoon in the middle of the island. The easiest way to hit them is to fly high above the island, then turn straight down and fly at the lagoon. When you've destroyed all the lagoon targets, finish off the bandits in the air and then follow your squad.

> **NOTE: THE PLANE YOU NEED TO FOLLOW SHOWS UP AS A FLASHING STAR ON YOUR RADAR.**

## Objective: Eliminate Japanese Carrier and Japanese Destroyer

The fun isn't over yet. Fly low and head for the red boxes on your radar. Either use your guns to destroy the ships or press Use to arm your bombs and Alt Fire to launch them.

Once you've sunk both boats, follow your squad toward the USS *Independence*. Before you actually make it there, though, you've got one more bogey to shoot down. Fly low and aim up at the plane chasing your teammate. Put a constant stream of bullets on the enemy to take him down.

## Objective: Land Safely Aboard the USS *Independence*

Make sure you've lined your plane up straight with the carrier as you fly in. Landing is easy. Just keep flying level at minimum speed, with the carrier directly in front of you, and you'll land safely.

## TARAWA

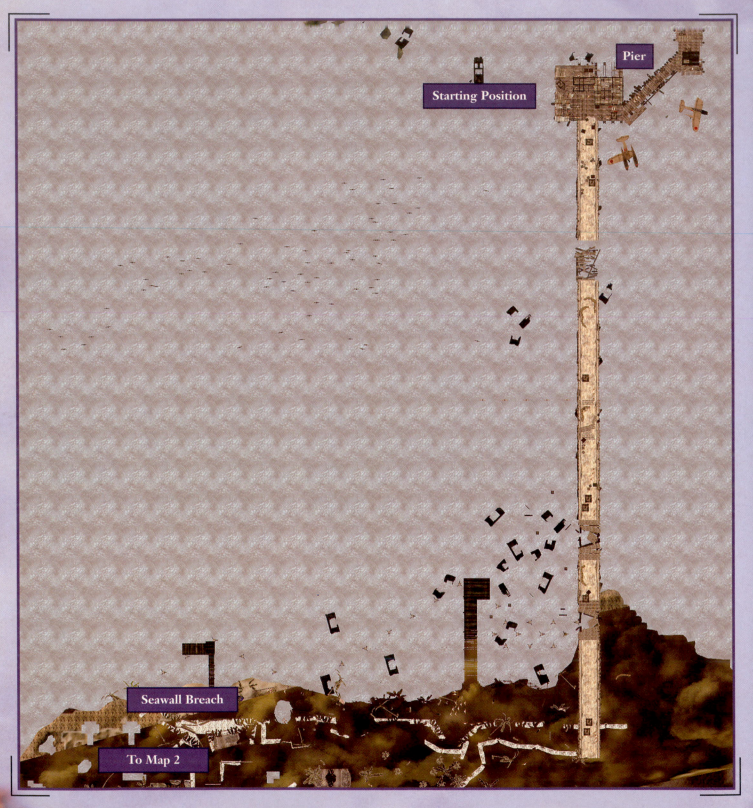

Starting Position

Pier

Seawall Breach

To Map 2

Gun Emplacement 4

Gun Emplacement 3

Gun Emplacement 2

Gun Emplacement 1

Map 2 Start

To Map 3

End Jeep Path

Start Jeep Path

Jeep

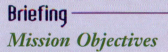

## Briefing

### Mission Objectives

- **Clear Enemies from the Pier**
- **Secure a Beachhead**
- **Locate and Cross Breach in Seawall**
- **Clear Remaining Structures on Red Beach 2**
- **Destroy Gun Emplacements Firing on LVTs**
- **Join Offensive at Red Beach 3**
- **Destroy the Gun Emplacements on Red Beach 3**
- **Neutralize the Bombproof Shelter**
- **Hold the Line and Eliminate the Remaining Defenders**
- **Defeat Final Banzai Charge**

## Available Weapons

- **BAR**
- **Riot Gun**
- **Arisaka**
- **M96 LMG**
- **Model 100 SMG**
- **M44 Carbine**

Gun 1

Gun 2

Map 3 Start

Gun 3

Gun 4

Gun 5

Gun 6

Gun 7

To Map 4

Map 4 Start

Friendly Tank

Final Battle

## Objective: Clear Enemies from the Pier

Take control of the machine gun and mow down the enemy soldiers on the pier to the left. When your boat reaches the pier, hop off and creep up the stairs to the next level. Stay low and clear out the soldiers on the right. Follow your teammate down to the lower level, then go back up the stairs on the other side of the gap. Creep up the stairs just like last time and take down the waiting soldiers.

> **TIP: SHOOT THE RED EXPLOSIVE BARRELS TO ELIMINATE SEVERAL ENEMIES AT ONCE.**

Walk down the stairs to find a portable machine gun and two health packs. Pick up the portable machine gun, then set it back down under the pier, pointing at the enemy soldiers at the far end. Gun them all down, then walk to the end of the pier and get back on your boat.

Climb up into the building's second story where the soldiers were hiding. Grab the ammo in the corner and use this spot to aim at the gunners in the boat below. Pick off both gunners, then climb back down and walk around to the back of the building.

## Objective: Secure a Beachhead

Use the machine gun on the boat to lay down a line of fire on the pier to the left. When the explosion rocks you out of the boat, immediately take cover behind the debris on the right. Pick off the soldiers hiding along the pier on the left. Stay covered as much as possible and wade to the beach to meet up with your squad.

> **TIP:** CHECK THE INSIDE CORNER OF THE DEBRIS FOR A HEALTH PACK.

## Objective: Locate and Cross Breach in Seawall

## Objective: Clear Remaining Structures on Red Beach 2

Stick with your squad and hug the left wall as you proceed. Eliminate the enemies in the way and keep moving. When you reach the bunker with the gunner inside, carefully peek around inside and fill him full of lead. Continue along the wall to find and finish off the remaining soldiers. Then, walk through the hole in the wall on the left.

Crawl through the trench to the right and peek around the corner. Pick off the soldier manning the machine gun and the others hiding behind the rocks and sandbags. Continue heading north and take down the soldiers in the building on the left. When you've cleared the building, check inside to find a portable machine gun.

> **NOTE:** THE PORTABLE MACHINE GUN'S FIREPOWER WILL HELP YOU, BUT CARRYING IT SLOWS YOU DOWN.

## Objective: Destroy Gun Emplacements Firing on LVTs

Follow your squad up onto the hill and eliminate the soldiers manning the machine guns inside the building. Then, walk into the building itself and look through the doorway on the east side to cap the soldiers waiting outside. Backtrack to the outside of the building and find the first gun emplacement to the south. Place an explosive charge to destroy it. The second is just a bit farther south. Set the charge and then meet your squad on the other side of the building.

Once you've cleared this area, turn around and head south. Look for the path to veer to the left, then get ready for more soldiers. If you're using the portable machine gun, set it down at the end of the path and mow down the opposition. Otherwise, stay covered along the wall and pick off each soldier. Continue around to the right and finish off the enemies hiding in the building to the south.

Head south and clear out the trench. When you've disposed of all the soldiers, find the next two gun emplacements along the right and blow them sky high.

Walk through the building on the right and find the trench behind it. Stick with your squad and follow the trench to the other side of the wall. More soldiers are on the other side, so get ready.

**TIP: LOOK INSIDE THE BUNKERS FOR AMMO.**

## Objective: Join Offensive at Red Beach 3

When you destroy the last gun emplacement, enemy gunners take position in the small gun bunkers on the hills. Carefully aim and nail each one, then find the door into the enemy's ammo depot in the wall to the southeast.

There are more enemies in here, so take 'em down. Find the red icon on the torpedo, then set an explosive charge and get out. Follow your squad over the wall and take on the enemy force on the other side. Aim through the crack in the building's wall to pick off the gunner inside. When your teammate starts the jeep, quickly press Use to hop in and ride to safety.

## Objective: Destroy the Gun Emplacements on Red Beach 3

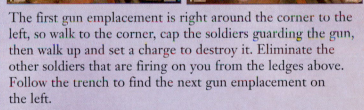

The first gun emplacement is right around the corner to the left, so walk to the corner, cap the soldiers guarding the gun, then walk up and set a charge to destroy it. Eliminate the other soldiers that are firing on you from the ledges above. Follow the trench to find the next gun emplacement on the left.

Follow your squad around the right side of the building to the east. When the enemies appear, backtrack and hole up inside the building. The window in the side is the perfect vantage point from which to gun down all the enemy soldiers as they run over the hill. After you've defeated them, head down into the trench and finish off the stragglers.

Follow the trench around to the right and head for the large building in the distance. You can't shoot the soldiers manning the machine guns, so stay covered and move forward only when they stop to reload. When you reach the building's wall, they can't hit you, so move along the wall and nail the enemies that run around the corner.

> **TIP: USE EXPLOSIVE CHARGES TO DESTROY THE TANKS.**

Peek into the door of the building and blast each soldier as he comes into view. Creep inside and finish off the survivors. Check the area for ammo, then rally with your squad and walk through the doorway that leads farther into the building.

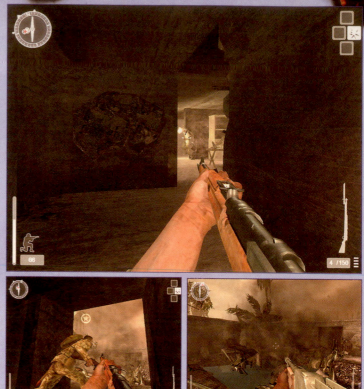

Cap the soldiers waiting in the room to the left, then move through the hall to the exit into the clearing. Gun down all the enemies that advance from the holes in the wall, then follow your squad around to the left.

Wade through the water and pick off the soldiers in the next hall. Continue through the hall until you reach open air. The next gun emplacement is just ahead to the right. Plug the soldiers guarding it, then move up and use your explosive charge to destroy it. The next gun is just to the left, so clear out the guards in the trench and destroy the gun.

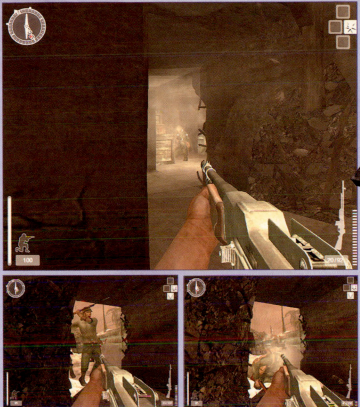

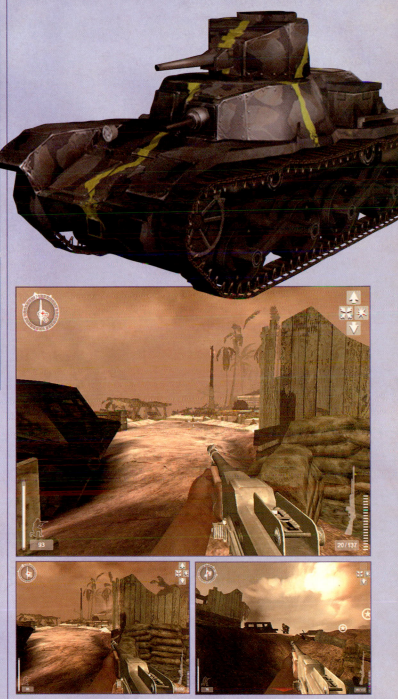

Head back into the building and walk through the new hall on the left. Drop the soldiers waiting in the next room and then move through and stop at the exit. There are lots of soldiers just outside the building, so hole up in the hallway and take them out one at a time.

The next gun emplacement is a little to the left, but there's also a machine gunner stationed to your right, on the ledge. Crawl along the wall on the right until you can look up over the ledge and quickly plug the gunner. Then, destroy the gun emplacement.

Follow the trench to find the next gun and blow it up.

The final gun emplacement is nearby to the northeast, guarded by a large group of soldiers. Follow your squad up onto the hill and take cover behind the corner. Poke your head out and pick off every soldier you can see. When you've cleared the area, move forward and eliminate any remaining soldiers. You can't hit the distant machine gunners, so stay covered as you approach the gun emplacement. Set a charge to destroy it.

## Objective: Neutralize the Bombproof Shelter

Follow the wall to the left and use the tank and bulldozer as cover to get to the shelter door on the left. Head into the shelter and stick with your squad. Follow the halls to the west and out into the clearing. Take out all the enemy soldiers and then climb out of the hole onto the upper ledge. Immediately take cover against the wall to the left.

Crawl along the wall and stop at the corner. You can't defeat the machine gunners on the left. Wait for a break in the firing, and then quickly run straight ahead to the top of the hill above the gunners. Find the red icon on the hilltop and set an explosive charge. Get clear of the explosion, but then return to the hilltop with your squad. Mow down the enemies that run in from the right and left. Then, head to the bottom of the hill and crawl around to the left. Finish off the rest of the soldiers holed up inside the shelter to complete the objective.

**TIP:** USE THE ENEMY'S MACHINE GUN TO TAKE THE SOLDIER DOWN.

## Objective: Hold the Line and Eliminate the Remaining Defenders

Drop the enemy soldiers as they run at you and your squad. Follow your men forward, and then hug the left wall as you continue. Cap the soldiers on the ridge in the distance, and then continue along the wall to the next trench.

Nail the machine gunner on the right and then proceed through the trench. There are more gunners on the ledges above you, so stay low. Continue creeping through the trench, stopping at each corner to scan for enemies.

**TIP: CHECK EACH BUNKER FOR AMMO.**

Follow your compass north through the trench until you move down into a room where the wall has been blown open. Use the wall as cover and plug the soldiers waiting in the clearing. When you can't see any more enemies from your current position, move up and use the truck in the clearing as cover.

**WARNING: THE SOLDIERS IN THIS AREA LOVE TO THROW GRENADES, SO BE READY TO RUN IF YOU SEE ONE FLY YOUR WAY.**

When you reach the dead end in the trench, wait for your friendly tank to show up and blow open a hole in the wall. Before you advance, use the edge of the trench on the left as cover and pick off the soldiers waiting on the left.

Follow your squad through the clearing and into the next trench. Stay low and near the wall so you can take cover when necessary. When you reach the enemy shelter, pick off every enemy within sight and move down into the trench to take cover. There are machine gunners in the walls of the shelter that you can't hit, so just stay down and wait for your teammate to radio for help.

## Objective: Defeat Final Banzai Charge

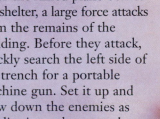

After the Allied plane bombs the shelter, a large force attacks from the remains of the building. Before they attack, quickly search the left side of the trench for a portable machine gun. Set it up and mow down the enemies as they run in. When every enemy soldier is on the ground, you complete your final objective. Good job, Marine.

77

## GAME TYPES

### Free For All

An FFA game is the most basic way to play a multiplayer game. As the name suggests, it's every man for himself in an attempt to score the most frags. Your initial choice of Allies or Axis determines which weapons you may choose. For a full list of the available weapons, refer to the Infantry/Heitai list in the Invader section.

### Team Deathmatch

Team Deathmatch is a fun alternative to Free For All. The difference is that you score points as a team instead of as an individual. You can spread out to cover more ground or stay together to tackle threats as a group. Spreading out reduces the speed with which you can take out a single target, but it also reduces the threat of walking into an ambush or losing everyone in the group to a grenade.

NOTE: AS IN FFA, THE TEAM YOU CHOOSE FOR TEAM DEATHMATCH DETERMINES YOUR CHOICE OF WEAPONS.

### Invader

An Invader game is far more complex (and fun) than a standard FFA or Team Deathmatch game. Not only do you choose a team, you must also choose a character class. Your class determines your available weapons and special abilities (as well as your job on the team). Once everyone has chosen their teams, the invading team must complete a series of objectives while the defending team fights them off.

## VOICE COMMANDS

Press V during any multiplayer game to bring up the Voice Commands menu. Use these commands to quickly issue orders or respond to requests by your team. For example, if you start an Invader game as a Corpsman and want to announce your presence, press V 4 2.

Memorize the lists here so you won't fumble with the keys in the heat of battle.

### Voice Commands

| Key | Command Type |
| --- | --- |
| 1 | General Requests |
| 2 | Class Requests |
| 3 | Commands |
| 4 | Replies |
| 5 | Talk |
| 6 | Voting |

### General Requests

| Key | Request Type |
| --- | --- |
| 1 | Under Fire |
| 2 | Cover |
| 3 | Reload Assist |
| 4 | Defend Objective |
| 5 | Take Objective |
| 6 | Defend and Hold |
| 7 | Direction |

### Class Requests

| Key | Request Type |
| --- | --- |
| 1 | Corpsman |
| 2 | Plant Explosive |
| 3 | Defuse Explosive |
| 4 | Plant Mines |
| 5 | Clear Mines |
| 6 | Ammo |
| 7 | Weapon |

### Commands

| Key | Request Type |
| --- | --- |
| 1 | Attack |
| 2 | Cease Fire |
| 3 | Take Cover |
| 4 | Advance |
| 5 | Follow |
| 6 | Fall Back |
| 7 | Scatter |
| 8 | Move |
| 9 | Finish Match |

### Replies

| Key | Request Type |
| --- | --- |
| 1 | Affirmative |
| 2 | State Class |
| 3 | Defending |
| 4 | Attacking |
| 5 | Negative |
| 6 | Thanks |
| 7 | You're Welcome |
| 8 | Apology |

## Talk

| Key | Request Type |
|-----|--------------|
| 1 | *Greeting* |
| 2 | *Compliment* |
| 3 | *Taunt* |
| 4 | *Insult* |
| 5 | *Congratulations* |
| 6 | *Cheer* |
| 7 | *Goodbye* |

## Voting

| Key | Request Type |
|-----|--------------|
| 1 | *Change Map* |
| 2 | *Change Gametype* |
| 3 | *Health Drop* |
| 4 | *Friendly Fire* |
| 5 | *Frag Limit* |
| 6 | *Time Limit* |
| 7 | *Mute Spectators* |
| 8 | *Kick Player* |

## INVADER GAME

### General Invader Notes

Just like in the single-player campaign, your compass always points toward your current objective. Colored boxes on the compass show the exact location of the object you need to interact with to complete the objective. If there are multiple objects, they show up as different colors on the compass. When your team is currently completing an objective (the charge is set but hasn't gone off, for instance), the colored box will flash.

Members from either team always spawn near the current objective. If your team is working on the final objective, you don't have to run across the entire map to rejoin your teammates when you die.

Explosive charges take 30 seconds to go off. Any time during those 30 seconds, the defending team can send an Engineer of their own to disarm the charge. Obviously, the invaders need to defend their charge to allow it time to detonate. This presents a new challenge, however, because the charge will damage anyone in the area when it goes off. To defend the explosive charge, remain close by and fight off the opposing team until the last few seconds, then stand clear. If you have a hard time keeping track of the 30-second time limit, use the spawn timer at the screen's upper right corner to count the seconds.

When taking on Destroy objectives, protect your Engineer as he sets the charge. If there are multiple objects to destroy and you have more than one Engineer on your team, send someone with each Engineer to protect them.

The objectives listed for each map refer to the invading team only. The defending team doesn't have any real objectives. Their job is simply to protect their own locations and prevent the invaders from succeeding.

Try to take an uncommon route toward the objective. If you always run up the same hill or crawl through the same hole, the defending team will have an easy time picking you off again and again. Split up your team when possible to confuse the defense.

## Classes

> **NOTE: ALL CLASSES SPAWN WITH A HANDGUN IN ADDITION TO YOUR CHOSEN WEAPON. ALLIED CLASSES HAVE A .45 MAGNUM WHILE THE AXIS HAS A NAMBU. THE ONE EXCEPTION IS THE ALLIED INFANTRY, WHICH SPAWNS WITH A COLT .45.**

### Allied: Infantry/Axis: Heitai

The Infantry class is an offensive powerhouse. They have the largest selection of weapons available (and are the only class that can choose a sniper rifle). The Infantry's sniping ability is a strong reason to take at least one on defense. On offense, however, you make survivability and objective completion your primary concerns. Take an Infantry class only if you have a large team with all your other bases covered.

### Available Weapons: Infantry

.30 Caliber M1 Carbine Rifle
M1 Garand
Springfield M1903 Rifle
Springfield M1903/A5 Sniper Rifle
M1928A1 Thompson SMG (With 50 Round Drum)
Reising Model 55 SMG
M1918A2 Browning Automatic Rifle (BAR)
Model 11 Remington Semi-Automatic Riot Gun

### Available Weapons: Heitai

Model 38 6.5mm Arisaka Rifle
Model 44 Cavalry Carbine Rifle
Model 97 6.5mm Sniper Rifle
Type 100 SMG
Model 96 6.5mm Light Machine Gun

## *Allied: Corpsman/Axis: Kangohei*

The Corpsman class has the unique ability to heal and revive their teammates. However, their weapon choice is limited to rifles. This makes them effective long-range fighters but leaves them relying on their sidearm. Still, a Corpsman is a very valuable (though not essential) member of any team.

### Available Weapons: Corpsman

.30 Caliber M1 Carbine Rifle
M1 Garand
Springfield M1903 Rifle

### Available Weapons: Kangohei

Model 38 6.5mm Arisaka Rifle
Model 44 Cavalry Carbine Rifle

## *Allied: Engineer/Axis: Kosakuhei*

The weapon choice of the Engineer is the exact opposite of the Corpsman. They are restricted to only close-range weapons. Thankfully, the Engineer class spends most of its time on the front lines because of its primary ability: the use of explosive charges.

On offense, at least one Engineer is mandatory on the team. Every map has at least one (but usually several) objects that you must destroy to complete the objectives. On defense, the Engineer is also the only class that can defuse enemy charges, thus preventing the enemies from completing their objective.

### Available Weapons: Engineer

M1928A1 Thompson SMG (With 50 Round Drum)
Reising Model 55 SMG
Model 11 Remington Semi-Automatic Riot Gun

### Available Weapons: Kosakuhei

Type 100 SMG
Model 96 6.5mm Light Machine Gun

## *Allied: Ammo Tech/Axis: Shichuhei*

The main job of the Ammo Tech class is to distribute ammunition for their team. However, they are the only class that can carry two primary weapons. Their selection of weapons is second only to the Infantry class. As a result, they have the unique ability to be powerful at long and close range by choosing a rifle and submachine gun. This makes the Ammo

Tech a jack-of-all-trades class that can handle almost any battle. On small teams, an Ammo Tech is more useful than an Infantry is.

### Available Weapons: Ammo Tech

.30 Caliber M1 Carbine Rifle
M1 Garand
Springfield M1903 Rifle
M1928A1 Thompson SMG (With 50 Round Drum)
M1918A2 Browning Automatic Rifle (BAR)

### Available Weapons: Shichuhei

Model 38 6.5mm Arisaka Rifle
Model 44 Cavalry Carbine Rifle
Type 100 SMG
Model 96 6.5mm Light Machine Gun

# Objective Types

There are four objective types. Keep in mind that there won't necessarily be one of each type of objective per map. Some objective types are more common than others.

## *Destroy*

This is the most common type of objective. Objectives of this type always involve destroying one or more objects by setting an explosive charge on the red icon. There is at least one of these objectives per map. Only Engineers can set explosive charges, so it's essential to have at least one on your team to succeed.

On defense, your job is two-fold. First, simply attempt to stop the invading team from reaching the objective point. If the invaders set the charge, you can still stop them by disarming the charge with your own Engineer.

## *Occupy*

Occupy is another very common objective type with at least one per map. To succeed at an Occupy objective, you simply need to stay in or near the target building or object for the given amount of time. You can move around and attack all you want as long as you don't leave the immediate area.

For the defending team, the only way to prevent the invaders from succeeding at an Occupy objective is to frag any player that approaches the target.

## *Operate*

Objectives of this type involve flipping a switch or using a radio. Flipping a switch is instantaneous, but the defending team can flip it back if they're fast enough. Using a radio has a timer bar like that of an explosive charge, so the defense can interrupt the invaders by fragging the man at the radio before he completes the broadcast.

## Collect

Collect objectives are found on only two maps, making them the least common type. An objective of this type is just what it sounds like; you must collect one or more objects from enemy territory to succeed.

Like an Occupy objective, the defending team must prevent the invaders from reaching the items. Most items take time to pick up, however, which gives the defense an extra bit of help.

## MAPS

These maps are also used in FFA and Team Deathmatch games. In those cases, simply ignore the objectives and map points.

## Airfield (Invaders: Axis)

- Objective: Disable Power Generator
- Objective Type: Operate

Enter the power generator building and flip the switch on the wall to begin the deactivation. Defend the switch for 20 seconds until the generator deactivates.

- Objective: Destroy Fuel Supply
- Objective Type: Destroy

Set an explosive charge on the fuel supply tank.

- Objective: Occupy the Support Building
- Objective Type: Occupy

Stand inside the support building for 15 seconds.

- Objective: Sabotage the Three Aircraft
- Objective Type: Destroy

Before you can reach the planes, you must set an explosive charge on one of the obstacles protecting the hangars. Once inside, set an explosive charge on each of the three planes. The target planes are each inside separate hangars.

## Bataan (Invaders: Allies)

- **Objective: Locate Codebook**
- **Objective Type: Collect**

Find the codebook in the back of the Axis caves. The specific location is random.

- **Objective: Neutralize Defensive Perimeter**
- **Objective Type: Destroy**

You must destroy five guns: three machine guns and two AA guns. Because each requires an explosive charge to destroy and an Engineer spawns with only four explosive charges, you're in a bit of a bind. Either take two Engineers or the one Engineer must die on purpose to respawn with four more charges.

- **Objective: Return to Amphibious Vehicle**
- **Objective Type: Occupy**

Return to your starting position at the beach. If the player carrying the codebook dies, it drops on the ground. If an Axis player touches the codebook, it returns to its starting position in the cave.

## Bougainville (Invaders: Allies)

- **Objective: Demolish 20mm Gun**
- **Objective Type: Destroy**

Set an explosive charge on the 20mm gun.

- **Objective: Destroy Roadblock**
- **Objective Type: Destroy**

Set an explosive charge on the roadblock.

- **Objective: Secure Beach Area**
- **Objective Type: Occupy**

Stand inside the bunker for 10 seconds.

- **Objective: Clear the Three Pillboxes**
- **Objective Type: Destroy**

Set an explosive charge on each of the three pillbox machine guns.

## Bridge (Invaders: Axis)

- **Objective: Destroy Heavy Machine Gun**
- **Objective Type: Destroy**

Set an explosive charge on the heavy machine gun.

- **Objective: Occupy Railroad Support Buildings**
- **Objective Type: Occupy**

Before you can actually get inside the support buildings, you must set an explosive charge on the outside wall. Once inside, you must stay inside the perimeter for 15 seconds.

- **Objective: Seize the Allied Patrol Base**
- **Objective Type: Occupy**

Stand anywhere inside the patrol base for 10 seconds.

- **Objective: Destroy Bridge**
- **Objective Type: Destroy**

Set an explosive charge on each of the two points on the bridge. Then move down into the valley below the bridge to find the detonator. Press Use to activate the detonator and destroy the bridge.

## Gavutu (Invaders: Allies)

- **Objective: Occupy the Water Cachement**
- **Objective Type: Occupy**

Stand near the water cachement for 30 seconds.

- **Objective: Gather Intel from the Wharf**
- **Objective Type: Collect**

Before you can reach the buildings where the intel is hidden, you must find a way into the compound. Either blow open the door with an explosive charge or go prone and crawl under the fence. Once inside, find the three pieces of intel in each of the three separate buildings.

- **Objective: Destroy the Two Mortars on Gaomi Island**
- **Objective Type: Destroy**

Set an explosive charge on each of the two mortars.

- **Objective: Transmit the Intel Back to Base**
- **Objective Type: Operate**

Find the radio inside the Axis building and transmit the intel.

## Gifu (Invaders: Allies)

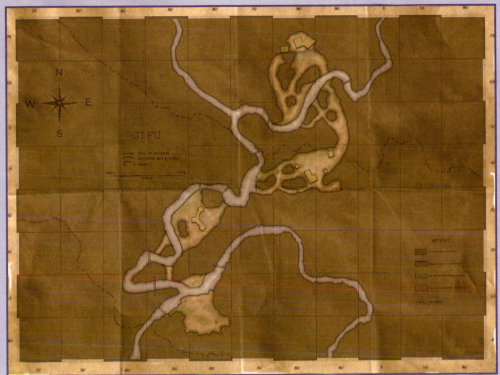

- **Objective: Occupy the Lookout Point**
- **Objective Type: Occupy**

Stand near the lookout point for 15 seconds. You do not need to climb up into it to satisfy the objective.

- **Objective: Destroy the Three Machine Gun Nests in the Gifu Bunkers**
- **Objective Type: Destroy**

Set an explosive charge on each of the three machine guns.

- **Objective: Control the Ammo Depot**
- **Objective Type: Occupy**

Stand inside the ammo depot for 15 seconds.

- **Objective: Turn On the Radio and Call In an Artillery Strike**
- **Objective Type: Operate**

Find the Axis radio building and use the radio to call in the strike.

## Mantanikau (Invaders: Allies)

- **Objective: Capture the Lookout Post**
- **Objective Type: Occupy**

Stand near the lookout post for 15 seconds.

- **Objective: Destroy the Two Bridge Barricades**
- **Objective Type: Destroy**

Set an explosive charge on each of the two bridge barricades. You must destroy the first to reach the second.

- **Objective: Secure the Weapons Cache**
- **Objective Type: Destroy**

Set an explosive charge inside the weapons cache.

- **Objective: Take Out the Three Anti-aircraft Guns**
- **Objective Type: Destroy**

Set an explosive charge on each of the three AA Guns. To reach the third, either set an additional charge on one of the two obstacles or crawl into the bunker under the hill.

## Wake Island (Invaders: Axis)

- **Objective: Destroy the Allied AA Gun on Wake Island**
- **Objective Type: Destroy**

Set an explosive charge on the AA Gun.

- **Objective: Destroy the Supply Ship at the Dock**
- **Objective Type: Destroy**

Set an explosive charge on the supply ship.

- **Objective: Occupy the Airfield Control Tower**
- **Objective Type: Occupy**

Stand near the control tower for 30 seconds. You do not need to climb up into it to satisfy the objective.

- **Objective: Activate the Runway Lights**
- **Objective Type: Operate**

Find and activate each of the two runway light switches.

# GLOSSARY

## ALLIES:

The Allies is the name given to the alliance of countries in opposition to the Axis Powers in World War II. The United States, Britain, France, Australia, New Zealand, India, the Soviet Union, Canada, and Greece are some of the countries that were part of the Allied Powers.

## AXIS:

The Axis powers consisted of Germany, Italy, and Japan as well as other nations strong-armed by Germany into the alliance. The three nations were not so much an alliance of ideology as they were an alliance of convenience. The reason that they were able to ally with each other was simply that their individual goals did not seriously conflict with each other.

## GUADALCANAL:

The fight for the island of Guadalcanal was the first battle to include an American amphibious invasion of Japanese-held territory. American forces launched the invasion on August 7 and landed near an unfinished airstrip that they quickly secured and renamed Henderson Field. They soon cleared out this area and it grew into an Allied staging area, which was reinforced with 17,000 Marines (even though it was constantly under fierce attack by Japanese forces). The Japanese launched a huge offensive against American forces at Guadalcanal in what became known as the Naval Battle of Guadalcanal. A Japanese naval force came toward the much smaller American task force and was able to sink two cruisers, but at the cost of a battleship. This led to American air raids, based off of Henderson Field, which were able to sink or badly damage all eleven transports stationed there. The Japanese came after American forces with all of their remaining naval units—four cruisers and a battleship. However, American forces sunk the battleship and two cruisers, which made it clear that the Japanese had failed to cause the American invasion forces to disengage. Jungle fighting continued on for another four months until American forces had secured the island in early February 1943.

## IWO JIMA:

The Battle of Iwo Jima was in early 1945 and was one of the fiercest and most costly battles of World War II. Between the Japanese and the U.S., over 25,000 lives were lost in the battle over this roughly 15 sq. mile island. Despite heavy bombardment for three months by the U.S. air force, the Japanese occupation forces at Iwo Jima held fast in their trenches. After a month of the most grueling combat in Marine history, the United States had secured the island at a cost of 6,000 American lives. However, the captured island served as the first U.S. air base close enough to Japan to allow medium bombers to execute bombing runs on the Japanese mainland.

## KAMIKAZE:

Kamikaze means "divine wind" in Japanese and refers to the suicide bombing runs made by Japanese pilots toward the end of the war. These attacks signified the last line of defense for the Japanese. Kamikaze pilots would take old warplanes and load them with explosives, and fly their planes directly into the hulls of American ships. The Japanese forces sank roughly 40 ships in this manner.

## MAKIN ATOLL:

Japanese forces occupied the island on December 9, 1941. United States Marines launched from a submarine during the night of August 17-18, 1942 and destroyed several flying boats and ships. This operation was the first Marine raid launched from submarines in history. Their mission was to destroy installations, disrupt the enemy, and divert reinforcements to Guadalcanal. After killing 83 Japanese and destroying installations, ships, and flying boats, the Marines had to evacuate in the face of Japanese air attacks and forces. While evacuating, they had to leave behind their dead, which the islanders and Japanese later buried in a mass grave.

## PEARL HARBOR:

Pearl Harbor is an inlet of the Hawaiian island of Oahu and is the site of one of the most important U.S. naval bases. On December 7, 1941, Japanese air units caught the U.S. naval base at Pearl Harbor by surprise with a sudden attack. Eighteen ships and over 200 planes were destroyed, and over 3000 people were injured or killed. This attack prompted the U.S. to enter the war on the side of the Allies to fight Japan and the Axis.

## SEPPUKU:

Seppuku is the term for Japanese ritual suicide. Many Japanese officers, to avoid the shame of surviving a lost battle, used ceremonial blades to kill themselves in the final days of many battles. These actions often led to great disorganization in the Japanese forces that remained and such forces were soon wiped out, with very few survivors.

## TARAWA:

This was one of the bloodiest battles between American and Japanese forces during World War II. The Japanese occupied Tarawa, one of the Gilbert Islands in the South Pacific, in 1942. As part of the Allied island-hopping campaign toward the Philippines, U.S. Marines bombarded the island, meeting heavy Japanese resistance but forcing an evacuation. In four days of fighting, 4,500 Japanese soldiers died, leaving fewer than 20 alive; 3,000 Marines were killed or wounded.

## WAKE ISLAND:

Wake Island was the site of a U.S. naval and submarine base during World War II. The Japanese invaded it immediately after the attack on Pearl Harbor on December 7, 1941. They were able to fight off the Japanese against overwhelming odds until December 23. The United States regained the island in 1945 when the Japanese surrendered and it is now under the control of the United States Air Force.

Here is a list of some of the phrases the Japanese soldiers yell during battle. They yell not only at you and your men, but also to each other to raise their spirits. Below is a phonetic pronunciation of the Japanese phrases, followed by the English translation.

## PRONUNCIATION GUIDE

Unlike in English, Japanese vowels are always pronounced the same way, no matter where in the word they are.

### Vowel Pronunciation

| Vowel | Pronunciation |
|-------|---------------|
| A | "ah" like the a in "father" |
| I | "ee" like the e in "we" |
| U | "oo" like the o in "soon" |
| E | "eh" like the e in "get" |
| O | "oh" like the o in "toe" |

| | |
|---|---|
| shine! | Die! |
| kono yaro! | You bastard! |
| sono choushi da! | Keep it up! |
| ii zo! | That's good! |
| ike! | Go! |
| tennou heika no tame da! | For the Emperor! |
| shouri ga mietekita zo! | Victory is in sight! |
| hirumu na! | Don't falter! |
| ketou o tsukamaero! | Capture the foreign dogs! |
| susume! | Advance! |
| shouri ga sugu soko da! | Victory is right before us! |
| tsukkome! | Charge! |
| yarareta! | I'm hit! |

## MARINE RANKINGS

### Enlisted

Private

Private First Class

Lance Corporal

Corporal

Sergeant

Staff Sergeant

Gunnery Sergeant

First Sergeant

Sergeant Major

### Officer

Second Lieutenant

First Lieutenant

Captain

Major

Lieutenant Colonel

Colonel

Brigadier General

Major General

Lieutenant General

General

## JAPANESE MILITARY RANKING

### Enlisted

Nitohei (Private)

Ittohei (Private First Class)

Jotohei (Superior Private)

Heicho (Lance Corporal)

Gocho (Corporal)

Gunso (Sergeant)

Socho (Sergeant Major)

### Officer

Shoi (Second Lieutenant)

Chui (First Lieutenant)

Taii (Captain)

Shosa (Major)

Chusa (Lt Colonel)

Taisa (Colonel)

Shosho (Major General)

Chujo (Lt General)

Taisho (General)

# HOW WILL YOU
# FIGHT THE BATTLE
## FOR MIDDLE-EARTH?

Middle-earth™ awaits your command. Develop your own real-time strategies to achieve victory in the epic battles of the film trilogy, then apply your warplans online. Whether you seek the One Ring or seek to destroy it, the fate of Middle-earth™ is in your hands. Begin the battle at eagames.com

THE LORD OF THE RINGS™
THE BATTLE FOR MIDDLE-EARTH™

THEY CAN TAKE AWAY YOUR LICENSE TO KILL
BUT NOT YOUR DESIRE

TRAINED AS AN ELITE MI6 AGENT YOU'VE BEEN EXPELLED FROM THEIR RANKS FOR YOUR

RECKLESSNESS AND BRUTALITY. NOW, AS A ROGUE AGENT, YOU'LL USE YOUR TRAINING

ALONG WITH AN ARSENAL OF OVER 100 TWO-FISTED WEAPON COMBINATIONS

TO SHOOT YOUR WAY TO THE TOP OF THE CRIMINAL UNDERWORLD.

YOUR SINGLE-PLAYER, SPLIT-SCREEN MULTI-PLAYER OR ONLINE

CRUSADE FOR VENGEANCE BEGINS AT EAGames.com